A Country
        North Wales

best wishes

Jan Miller
      (née Klein)

Jan Miller

A Country Diary
for
North Wales

Matador
9 De Montfort Mews
Leicester LE1 7FW, UK
Tel: (+44) 116 255 9311 / 9312
Email: books@troubador.co.uk
Web: www.troubador.co.uk/matador

ISBN 1 905237 35 9

Cover illustrations: Alan Wagstaff

Typeset in 11pt Stempel Garamond by Troubador Publishing Ltd, Leicester, UK
Printed in the UK by The Cromwell Press Ltd, Trowbridge, Wilts, UK

Matador is an imprint of Troubador Publishing Ltd

In memoriam; Alan Christopher Wagstaff, 1970 to 2005

He made everyone's efforts feel worthwhile and shared his appreciation of the natural world with easy humour and pleasure.

Contents

Introduction

This little book began life as a monthly nature diary in the Denbighshire Free Press; in this regular local newspaper column I try to help people look at already familiar things as well as the unfamiliar around them in the countryside and find new beauties. I also want to keep up to date with the current state of the environment in North Wales and put people in touch with the local organisations and clubs that are working to protect the local wildlife as well as showing the public where to see it. Each month includes contact details for the organisations and local events mentioned. There is also an appendix at the end of the book that lists these together with many more. If you have any suggestions to add to this list for a future edition, please e-mail them to; info@northwalesbutterflies.org.uk

In February 2005, my good friend and fellow volunteer with the North Wales Branch of Butterfly Conservation, Alan Wagstaff died of cancer at the heartbreakingly early age of 34. He had been a prolific wildlife artist, designing most of the Reserve guide leaflets for the North Wales Wildlife Trust and making interpretation panels for national reserves like the Great Orme. His family agreed it would be a nice tribute to him to use some of his line drawings and paintings in this book; I hope he would approve of their setting.

We had a garden party for my husband's birthday last summer, and a number of people said how beautiful the garden looked—one even said the herbaceous border was "stunning". I hadn't noticed—of course I had worked frantically for the week before pulling out the couch grass, buttercups and nettles, as well as hastily planting in ready-meals of blue delphiniums and pink cone-flowers in the obvious gaps, to try and make it look OK enough. But you get so used to your own creations that you stop seeing them. Funny how you can visit someone else's garden or house and be charmed by a simple arrangement of steps with pots of flowers or pictures on a wall that the person who lives with it never notices anymore. I tried to sit at the end of my 'stunning' border with a glass of wine in the evening sun the day after the party and just *see* it—but it was very difficult. All I could see was that group of nettles or dandelions I really should have dug out. I hope this book might help some readers to find the beauty and wonder in the everyday things as well as the special.

I have started the diary in the more propitious September rather than the traditional January because it's a warmer place to start appreciating the countryside.

Jan Miller
Whitford, May 2005

Acknowledgements

Thanks are due to Alan Wagstaff's family for allowing use of his drawings and paintings, to Philip Snow for the drawing of newts, to Alice Wakefield for her poem, to Rob Whitehead for proof reading and information, to Miller-Klein Associates for sponsorship, to Butterfly Conservation staff and volunteers who have taught me so much and to all the many naturalists I have met over the years who have generously shared their knowledge with me.

September

Autumn is my favourite time of year. The gorgeous tree colours won't come yet 'til after the first frost, but on a sunny day now, for only two or three weeks, there's an unearthly stillness with that Golden Syrup quality of light, and the temperature is just perfect. Long shadows, russet colours of fruit and flowers, the sweet smell of decaying vegetation. Everything is slowing down to a peaceful maturity before the long winter sleep.

Chunky toy umbrellas of fungi sprout all over the woods, helping to recycle the decay; yellow, white and brown on their fat stalks. Small markers of secret, extensive underground threads doing their silent work.

Many animals are busy fattening up for hibernation through, or migration from, the famine of winter. Goldfinches come especially to thistles and teasels for the protein-packed seeds. (Thistle seed feeders are available from local garden centres). A flash of yellow bands on their wings as they fly up before you, a red stripe mask across their faces. Some birds feed up on insects; 2003 was an exceptional summer for butterflies. But many in gardens in such long, hot seasons—Painted Ladies, Red Admiral and Silver Y moth, and Hummingbird Hawkmoth, have flown in from the continent and won't survive the winter here. The true natives like Small Coppers—dainty little flitting orange wings with black dots on the Yarrow, and Common Blues, blue like a summer sky, on the Bird's Foot Trefoil, and clouds of Small Tortoiseshells on the Michaelmas Daisies in my butterfly border are stocking up on sugar too. It seems to be the species that have two broods a year have done best, but unusually there was a *third* generation of Tortoiseshell caterpillars on my nettles in 2003.

A badger snuffles around the base of my bird table at 11.30 each night—he has learnt there are good pickings dropped by careless birds during the day. Reptiles too are using the last warm days to activate their bodies to catch that last mouse—digesting slowly, just one can see them through several months. Only four reptiles in this area; Grass snake, Adder, Slow worm (really a legless lizard) and Common Lizard, as well as the rare Sand Lizard recently re-introduced near Talacre. They are handsome creatures—smooth and golden with dashed stripes of dark brown all down their lithe backs. All are very shy and thus rarely seen. On Moel Findeg looking for them; several corrugated iron squares had been laid amongst the heather—reptiles like to hide under the ridges and glean warmth from the sun-heated metal. We were warned; "if bitten by an Adder (very rare) don't run— just sit down and use your mobile phone and GPS (satellite

Common lizard by Alan Wagstaff

2

positioning device) to call for help"—eeh, when I were a lass....!
Such technology was unimaginable then.

Why do people hate snakes? D.H. Lawrence hauntingly describes
an encounter; 'And trailed his yellow-brown slackness soft-bellied
down'. He tells us how honoured he felt to have such a guest.
And really we do see so little of our wonderful wildlife—most
hides from us in fear. He also says "If a man was as much a man
as a lizard's a lizard, he would be worth looking at."

More information

Fungal Forays with North Wales Wildlife Trust; tel;01352 810469
and Denbighshire Council Countryside Service; tel;01352 810614
Also other local societies often run autumn fungal forays, eg. Llanarmon yn
Ial Conservation Soc. and Dyserth Field Club
NEWW (Deeside Urban Wildlife Group) and CCW courses on amphibians
and reptiles; see appendix
Butterfly Conservation lectures on Gardening for Butterflies and Moth
Identification; tel 01352 711198, website; www.northwalesbutterflies.org.uk

Quotations
D.H.Lawrence's poems "Snake" and "Lizard".

Have you ever experienced the thrill of cracking open a rock
and finding a fossil inside that hasn't seen the light of day for
millions of years? We have two great belts of limestone that run
roughly north-south in Flintshire and Denbighshire where you
can do just that. You don't even have to crack them open—
often fossils can be found just lying around on the floor of any
of the disused quarries in the area. Eglwyseg Rocks, at the
southern end of the county, dominate the landscape above
Llangollen like giant white standing surf crashing up an ancient
beach, frozen in time. Like the rest of our limestone ridges, they
date from the Carboniferous period—about 350 million years
ago, when this part of Britain lay under a shallow sea in sub-
tropical temperatures, so coral reefs built up just like the Great

Barrier Reef off Australia today. But the fossils you will find here are of extinct species—though recognisably related to modern ones; huge shapes like giant cockle shells (called Brachiopods) varying from about 3 inches to 8 inches across, or sections through them, looking like pale crescent moons against the darker grey background of the rock. Also many circular or tubular sections, about a quarter of an inch diameter and divided into ribs with a central hole—these are pieces of the tall stems of the so-called "Sea lilies". They were not actually plants, but coral-like animals that lived in the top tentacular head of the "lily flower"—their technical name is Crinoid. It's very rare to find the "head", but the little tubular sections of stem frequently weather out from the rock—I once had a friend who threaded them on a necklace. Not very pretty, but a great conversation opener! The actual corals of the fossil reefs are rather more difficult to find. They can look similar to the Crinoids, but the way to tell the difference is they have very fine lines radiating out from a central column, and no central hole.

The Denbighshire Walking Festival in September included a trip to Eglwyseg Rocks and geological tour around Llangollen itself. Towns are great places to see good examples of fossils and minerals in the polished stone facings of buildings like banks and supermarkets much more clearly than in the field. I used them to teach my children the basic rock types when they were little— when we walk past a building now I just have to say "OK, what's this?" and they resignedly drone "Granite, Mum" or whatever it happens to be. They seem rather fed up with it. But I hope they will discover it to be a useful skill one day.

The Geodiversity Officer (yes, new one on me too) guided us to the only remaining building in Llangollen built of local limestone -the old Armoury, and it's stuffed with fossils. This rock seems to have been too crumbly to be good for building, however, and most used the local grey mudstone. Expensive decorative polished rocks were used sparingly, like the pink granite pillars framing the Town Hall door or the Serpentine legs of the church font. We were given a good tip—when you can't see an outcrop of local rock, look at the walls along the road. They will usually have been made with the stones found just there. We even discovered volcanic bombs—lava projectiles the size and shape of rugby balls—from ancient Ordovician eruptions, in one Llangollen wall.

In the Churchyard is the tomb of the celebrated Two Ladies of Llangollen—the rock for their side is marble, but the slab for their servant on the other side is ordinary limestone. For all their eighteenth century liberalism (they appear to have been a Lesbian couple who eloped together) and intellectuality (they entertained Dr. Johnson, the Duke of Wellington and many other worthies of the day)—they still drew the line at social equality!

Carboniferous Limestone fossils all found in Flintshire and Denbighshire—top and left Giagantoproductus shells and right, corals. (The 2p. piece is for scale)

Look out for

RIGS (Regionally Important Geological Sites) publish geological guides to a number of local towns; contact the Geodiversity Officer, c/o Millennium Ecocentre, Borras Airfield, Tarmac, Holt Road, Wrexham LL13 9SE.
Tel; 01978 361543, e-mail j.malpas@chester.ac.uk Website; www.ukrigs.org

To get to Eglwyseg Rocks, turn up hill by the Bridge End Hotel in Llangollen, then turn right up Wern Road and follow up narrow lanes to the foot of Dinas Bran. Car parking, lots of tracks to drive along and paths to walk.

The Ladies of Llangollen by Elizabeth Mavor is a fascinating read.
Their wonderful, eccentric house, called Ty Newydd, is now a National Trust property and can be visited near by Llangollen.

October

Every year I am surprised by the variation in the seasons. Several years ago I wrote on the calendar "September 4th—best blackberries"; a couple of years ago they weren't ready even a month later and another year I had friends eating their first blackberry and apple crumble in August. Wild flowers in recent winters, when walking with the Dyserth and District field Club surprised us—finding several spring and summer flowers—buttercup, hedge-parsley and scarlet pimpernel still flowering in October and into November. Were they fooled by global warming, or just showing the normal cyclical variation in our climate? Global warming is generally accepted now, and it's not going to get any colder, whatever we do; the task is to stop it getting any warmer. But still we can get frequent extremes, up and down, as probably has always happened in this island surrounded by sea. Many native species will suffer if the general trend is much warmer, however.

Another environmental topic that has become political is genetically modified (GM) crops A lot of people have an emotional instant reaction to this subject—but, as with most things in life, there's no clear "good" or "bad" about it. A DEFRA report has been produced on the four years of trials to find out just how much they would affect the environment. Encouragingly, it is the first time that such a huge amount of money and effort has been spent on finding out just what we are doing to our natural environment, and lots of things have been discovered, not just how GM crops affect it. Three types of crop were trialed, and all had a gene inserted to make them resistant to the weedkiller to be used around them. At first this sounds alarming, but the report says that with the Maize crop (only grown for cattle fodder in this country) the numbers of wildflowers, insects and birds (altogether part of the "biodiversity") actually increased. This is because the crop only needed to be sprayed later, and with a weaker herbicide than the conventional crop is normally, so the weeds grew better at the critical time for insects, and birds fared well on them. The GM Oilseed Rape and Sugar Beet crops, however, had to be sprayed at a different time and the biodiversity amongst them was lower than in the conventional crops. The implication is that GM crops that encourage less wildlife will not get approved. Rape seed oil is being used, amongst other things, to replace the oils we used to get from whale fat, so I am always glad to see those waving blocks of bright lemon-yellow fields in summer, in the knowledge that they are helping to save the whales.

We quite often see buzzards wheeling overhead nowadays—you can hear their plaintive "mew, mew" from high above -they are said to be on the increase. And in recent years I have seen more dead polecats, otters and badgers beside the road than ever before; there are plenty of badger latrines in the woods—pits about 5 inches long, and nearly as deep, filled with dark brown chipolata droppings. Farming is in serious trouble in Wales at the moment, but perhaps the unexpected blessing is that wildlife is returning, and thank goodness the increased public concern about the environment is forcing our government to really take notice—like conduct trials and make reasoned decisions. We may well end up with some GM crops being banned and not others—in future developments, some could be fantastically useful, like growing medicines and other products that at present have to be extracted from animals, and doing it very cheaply, whilst giving farmers another source of income; so don't let us throw the baby out with the bathwater.

The sloes are fat and plentiful this year—promising cosy Christmas nights around the fire sipping Sloe gin. I have an old recipe for 'Hedge-row jam', using hips, haws and sloes as well as the usual blackberries and crab apples. You have to strain away the pulp, of course, but these normally untasted free fruits are supposed to give an extra mysterious flavour. I always mean to try it, perhaps one year I will.

Recipe for Hedgerow Jam

2Kg. wild fruits of your choice (Sloes, Bilberries, Elderberries, Rose Hips, Haws, Blackberries, Crab Apples or Cooking Apples)
(those ripening earlier than the others (eg. Elderberries) can be frozen until the others come into season. Don't get them confused with the vines of bright red and yellow poisonous Bryony berries on our winter hedges.)
Sugar (same weight of sugar as cooked fruit pulp)
Water

Remove stalks and leaves and cut apples into quarters. Put all the fruit into a pan with water to barely cover and gently simmer until soft (about 30 minutes). Put through a sieve. Weigh pulp and return to pan with equal weight of sugar. Stir to dissolve sugar and bring to the boil. (If you want a clear jelly instead of jam, leave it to drain through a fine cloth or jelly bag without pressing, overnight.) Then boil hard until the jam reaches setting point (crinkles on cold saucer). Pot, cover and seal.

More information
Reports on the GM crop trials can be viewed on; www.defra.gov.uk

I was speaking at a conference on wildlife gardening and Bob Flowerdew (he of organic fame) was also there. Gosh he was good—I do admire someone who can just stand up at the front and chat away for the exact appointed time, without the assistance of projectors, Powerpoint presentations or anything else except his own skill with words. He enthralled the audience with such statistics as "a hedgehog travels about three miles in a night, slugs and snails only about twenty feet"—the implication being that if you plant further than twenty feet away from the slugs favoured habitat, at the same time as encouraging hedgehogs and other gastropod predators into the garden you won't need to worry. His whole thesis was 'get the wildlife to do the gardening for you'. He spoke about companion planting and how everything in the garden affects everything else there. Of course, getting the balance just right is what a lot of us find difficult—and this becomes even more important in the wider countryside. As I flew into Vienna airport I enjoyed looking out of the window at the land below spread like a map—an undulating patchwork quilt on a broad bed, divided by rivers and clumps of woods. But it was dramatically obvious that intensive farming around the city had meant the loss of hedges and corridors of woodland. When we visited country areas around the city I noticed not one single butterfly—not even a wasp (I know it was getting cooler, but we still had insects in North Wales a month later.) Whether you like them or not, insects tell us a lot about the healthy balance of the local ecology—and the only birds I heard or saw were a couple of Jackdaws scavenging from bins in the city. Worrying.

Another thing I saw there was a number of smallish wind farms (typically with only about 4 or 5 windmills). They tell me they've had them for quite a bit longer than we have, and there wasn't a problem with them going up, but there is now with some that need to come down. Apparently this wasn't thought about when the windfarms were constructed; now some of them have come to the end of their useful life and no-one wants to take responsibility for their de-construction—sometimes the land they are on now even has a different owner. And it costs a lot to dismantle those giants! Maybe something for our windfarmers to keep in mind. But I must say they do look beautiful—those towering formation teams like some white-suited retro Motown singers flinging their arms up to the sky together—they can only enhance the landscape, as far as I can see, especially some of our bleak moorlands. People love the Angel of the North, why don't they like windmills?

When the lines of Dutch windmills were first built along dykes to pump water from the polders in the sixteenth century there was an outcry from local worthies then. Imagine if you had never seen any industrial machinery, what monstrosities they must have seemed! Now of course tourists flock to photograph their stately beauty. It's all about perspective and balance. If government is finally listening to us about seriously addressing global warming, and trying to balance the ecology, it seems rather churlish to turn round now and say we don't like the view. In any case, when some improved technology for other renewable energy becomes viable these windfarms will mostly disappear. Nothing is permanent in our landscape. Except perhaps the slugs and snails!

November

You can still toil up the hill where the poet Gerard Manley Hopkins caught that morning, more than 130 years ago, the sight of the "Windhover" riding on the level air. Up the lane from St. Beunos, where he was in training for the Jesuit priesthood, at Tremerchion. The steep banks and hedges tower darkly over the wet tarmac (springs pop out all over the slopes in this wet season), and suddenly open through a 5-bar gate onto moorland and smooth, sweeping, rounded fields, dipping down to the valley. The wide rift of the rivers Clwyd and Elwy, where Hopkins followed the 'hurrahing in of the harvest' leads the eye up over to the mountains of Snowdonia that often used to be snow-capped at this time of year, but recent Novembers have been too mild. Unfortunately, the valley itself is now scarred by a deep, gray gash where the new A55 sections the Silurian slates—releasing millions of years of overburden pressure so that they are trying to spring free as if from a card sharp's thumb-flicked deck. Ugly great bolts and draping tar blankets are straining to hold them down.

But, turning back over the shoulder of the hill, you can imagine yourself back in Hopkins' time. Birds of prey wheel overhead, sometimes mirrored by white gliders, and walking past munching sheep you come to a little stone chapel hidden in the trees. Dark green conifer spaces beckon down the other side of the hill, and you emerge at the tranquil monks' graveyard and orchard, by the Victorian college building, which is now used as a retreat.

The national Hopkins' society is run from nearby. They have an annual lecture and workshops on Hopkins' poetry. They are sometimes given a tour of St. Beuno's, and take the walk over the hill.

Local volunteers, aided by a grant from the Countryside Council for Wales, have begun their winter work on clearing scrub from the Eyarth Rocks Reserve near Ruthin. A beautiful crisp sunny day last Wednesday found us sawing hawthorn and gorse trunks off the limestone pavement; exposing anew this special bit of the habitat that is home to a number of rare plants. The undulating view over to the purple Clwydian Hills was dotted with sheep against verdant green fields on the lower slopes. The Pearl-bordered Fritillary butterfly that still breeds here, one of the rapidly dwindling number of sites in the UK, needs to feed on Dog Violet (*Viola riviniana*) as a caterpillar in March and April, earlier than most other native species. For this it needs extra warmth provided by thin, dry soils on east or south-facing slopes surrounded by bracken that shelters it. However, if the old dead bracken forms a layer more than 15cm. it smothers the violets—as does dense, encroaching scrub; the foodplant disappears and the butterfly can only fly less than a mile to try to find another habitat. Sheep used to graze these areas, but now it's not economic for the farmers to use this marginal land. In the wild forest there would have been dying trees every few miles and natural clearings where the right conditions existed for a few years before the habitat specialists like this butterfly had to move onto the next suitable patch. It seems most endangered species are the ones that find their niche in a transient special habitat like this. We have lost the diversity of habitat so we are losing the diversity of life—unless we step in to create the habitat artificially.

Driving home with music playing and the sun slanting low through the narrow trees at the side of the road, the light caught on many orange-glow-brown leaves double spiralling up in the wake of the lorry wheels in front of me—they looked for a moment very like some of the rare butterflies we are trying to save up on Eyarth Rocks.

I enjoyed watching those leaves in time to the music all the way up the hill—the one that mirrors another massive Silurian slate slope at such an acute angle that I often wonder how on earth a tractor can get up it. We volunteers for the local branch of Butterfly Conservation got some great free exercise in the fresh air, in a much prettier location than the local gym, as well as a cheering bonfire and a sense of virtuous satisfaction in our tired limbs when we climbed into that hot bath with a glass of wine once home at the end of the day.

More information

Hopkins Society, secretary; I. Jones, 41 North Drive, Rhyl LL18 4SW, tel; 01745 354 151 www.hopkinsoc.freeserve.co.uk

If you would like to help with conservation work, from November to March at Eyarth Rocks Reserve, or would just like more information about the Reserve, go to www.northwalesbutterflies.org.uk or telephone 01352 711198.

Pearl-bordered Fritillary (photo – R. Whitehead)

Notwithstanding the occasional bit of snow, we've been having remarkably mild Novembers. Remember when we were children at Bonfire Night parties? You spent half the time hugging the fire while your bum froze, and the other half trying to thaw out your rear while your breath misted the dark air with white frost. For quite a few years now our children have stood around in their shirt sleeves to watch the garden fireworks. The mildness has meant many plants that used to be long ago abed are still flowering—picking blackberries in mid-November, not only were there still a few flowers on the bushes, but there were new flower buds forming too.

And up on Eyarth Rocks Reserve the fungi were still out in all their finery. Fungi are not flowering plants, but the toadstools are their 'fruiting bodies'—it's how they reproduce. Underground miles of fine white or black threads join the mushrooms together, and it's these threads, or mycelia, together with worms and bacteria, that are breaking down all the waste materials to make new soil. Nature's own recycling centre.

Hopping from foot to foot across the hopscotch natural limestone pavement, the deep green grikes hiding ferns and dwarfed trees in their depths, the wind whipped stray hairs across eyes and cheekbones. Limestone pavement is rare in Britain. It forms when the rock is just the right kind of density to withstand weathering, leaving cubic slabs standing proud above the square gridwork of joints carved downwards by the rain. Lots of our limestone in north-east Wales is criss-crossed underneath too with tunnels and shafts, like mycelia, where until quite recently there was mining for lead. These minerals weren't in the original Carboniferous limestone; they came later, in percolating solutions through cracks and faults—the far-end ripples of the Alpine mountain building period.

Happily Eyarth Rocks escaped much mineralization and so

Fly Agaric fungi, from an original painting by Alan Wagstaff.

weren't mined to destruction. Down in damp hollows where a moss and lichen tapestry carpet has grown with the wetter weather of recent years, nestled amongst the glowing velvet green were many clusters of little scarlet fungal wax caps—said to be indicators of ancient, undisturbed grassland. The aptly named "Brain Fungus" looked just like someone had spilt fresh, glistening scrambled egg on the rotting gorse branches. Nice chunky, cream, squat fellows clustered together between browned bracken fronds and elegant flutes of palest grey looked almost as if Art Deco wine glasses had been set out on the green cloth for a picnic. The diversity of colours and shapes among fungi is amazing—why should they bother to be so different and beautiful when they don't need to attract insects to pollinate them or birds to eat them? Maybe it, and the poison inside many, is to warn animals not to eat, as the spores would then be destroyed. Unlike hard berry seeds which need scarifying through a gut before germinating in a new-dropped place with their own package of manure. The wind is all the fungi need to blow their fine-as-dust ripe spores away to the next recycling centre. Up on the windswept limestone cliff there was no better illustration of the difference between our gardened and our wild landscapes, as the ancient Welsh poet Pedrog observed;

> *A crystal home the rose was given, its soft*
> *Gentility to pamper;*
> *For brave heather, rock suffices —*
> *The bare republic of the wild.*

The small group of Friends of Pistyll Gwyn Quarry, not far away at Llanarmon yn Ial, are hoping to help the disused quarry to become another limestone nature reserve. They welcome new members.

Look out for

Friends of Pistyll Gwyn Quarry, Sec. tel; 01824 780684, or john@shakesby1.fsnet.co.uk

Learn more about fungi from; www.fungus.org.uk and go to North West Fungus group (including Denbighshire and Flintshire)

Welsh Verse, Translations by Tony Conran, published by Seren

December

Don't you think our wild trees are almost more beautiful in winter than they are in summer? I love those giant skeletons throwing their great, dendritic arms against the sky as if holding massive fishing nets to filter the wind. In Canada I've walked through winter woods after freezing rain when all the little twiglets are encased in ice, and they tinkle in the wind above you like clouds of tiny bells.

You don't get these dramatic transformations in the Tropics, of course—trees there are in a constant cycle of flowering and fruiting and in leaf all year round. But unlike in the rainforests, we are losing our woods in this country because we are *not* cutting them down. All of the remaining forests of Wales together would now only fill the Isle of Anglesey. And the woods we do have left are often not being managed for their products anymore. This means that all the trees are growing old and dying together—shading out any new seedlings that try to come up from below. Coed Cymru is an organisation that is helping farmers to re-instate some of the old traditions of forestry, including selected felling for timber, coppicing for the rods used in garden furniture and fencing, and charcoal production. The harvesting of the woodland's gifts means that new clearings are opened up to sunlight—this not only helps the regeneration of the woodland itself from the tree seeds, but also gives life to wild flowers and the insects and birds that feed on them. In fact, Man's using the forest can increase its biodiversity enormously.

Peter Boyd is a local craftsman who makes use of felled or fallen trees. He was often told he had his head in the clouds, and now he does, literally. Living on the slopes of Snowdonia, where Welsh myths merge in the mists that swirl over grey-blue slate, heather-brown and purple moorland, he has his wood-carving workshop in the outbuildings of an old stone farmhouse. Brown ochres of wood glow, breaking through from the rough bark, as the sun breaks through the mist spotlighting a towering corrie, the oil on the wood spotlights a gnarly knot of elm, sectioned to reveal rings and circles and glowing grain.

Peter makes mirror-frames, furniture and other artifacts in a very individual style, reminiscent of the Spanish artist Gaudi—organic, flowing forms that follow the natural features in the wood, one root flows into an eye, one lock of luxuriant hair flows into a Moorish arch—follows the grain, follows the gleam. All are carved by hand. "I know a few wood-workers who use power tools almost exclusively" says Peter "but I like to work by hand; there's something fundamental in creative work about getting in touch directly with your material".

Peter started out with a psychology degree and then taught people with learning difficulties in an art-therapy community in Chester. He was interested in understanding human creativity, and how people with mental disorders are often very creative. But he felt constrained, there was a lot of medication and containment of the patients, and it was stressful; after three years he wanted to get away. He travelled in North America and worked on farms in the arctic, including using a pole-lathe and working with greenwood. Fascinated by Native American culture, he spent a year following a course on their lore and craftwork; this re-inforced his interest in wood. "The Native Americans have a lot of respect for trees" says Peter "they say there are five tribes; the red (themselves), the white, yellow, brown and the 'standing'—these are the trees"

Meanwhile Peter's mother had taken on a small-holding in

Peter Boyd and his woodcarving.

North Wales and Peter went to live there to help out when he returned. He learned joinery skills in doing renovation work on the buildings, while practising his woodcarving. Eventually he achieved his dream of going into woodcarving full-time, and obtaining a property in a wonderfully inspiring location, near other craftsmen, where he and now his wife and four children could live creatively.

Peter is very aware of the ecological problems we are facing with the loss of woodland, and most of the trees he uses are ones that shouldn't have been cut down but were removed because of building work, for example. He feels it is a positive action to take this "dead body" and make something of value that people respond to. "This is a time of great change" says Peter "we are moving out of an industrial and patriarchal age, and it's an important time to express what that change is. I like to think that my mirrors are like a gateway, and we look through to see what is on the other side." He feels that working with natural materials is an antidote to technological advance, and the popularity of his work is testament to other peoples' yearning for this antidote too. Peter has a six-month waiting list on his commissions, and displays his work at a dozen craft fairs around Britain each year.

He also runs courses in wood-carving in his workshop; small numbers of people can stay on his misty mountain and learn skills and absorb themselves in the creative atmosphere for three days or so. My own family have been several times—with two teenage sons, the eldest having Asperger's Syndrome and starting when the youngest was only ten. Peter tailored the course to our needs, and we each came away with a product we were proud of and a feeling of peace and satifaction; some people might say, with our heads in the clouds.

Ivy is a great plant in the woods. Some people don't like ivy on their trees, but it is actually a myth that it kills them like a

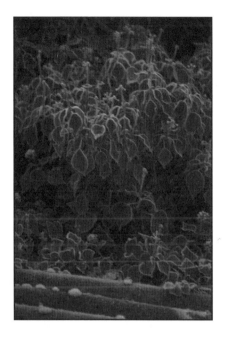

Ivy with hoar frost

parasite, though it can reduce the vigour of the tree by simple weighing down and smothering. Some judicious pruning by cutting through the bigger ivy stems at ground level can control this. Holly and ivy had an association with the pagan solstice celebrations long before Christianity took over this time of year. Perhaps because they were the only plants that were a healthy green in the depths of winter. And our native ivy is still the latest to flower, in spite of all our foreign garden imports. Ivy only flowers in its second stage of growth, so if you keep cutting it back you won't see the pretty pom-poms of pale greenish yellow all over in November, providing scarce nectar for any insects that may still be around in a warm spell. It's also important for hibernation and nesting sites.

23

I don't know if it's something to do with the solstice, but the weather often seems to change just around Christmas Day. We may have snow before and snow afterward, but Christmas itself is often clear, crisp and sunny. As a child I always regretted the way we wasted those few sunny hours with waiting for and wading through Christmas dinner at lunch-time; it would be nearly dark by the time we'd finished. So with my own family we often put the turkey in after we've done the presents and then jump in the car and head for Snowdon. It's surprisingly crowded there on Christmas Day—even hard to find a space in the car park.

One year it was pouring with rain, but we still went on principle. The kids refused to get out of the car "You're mad!" they shouted after their dad and me as we ran up the start of the Miners' Track. We met some people coming down "Happy Christmas!" we called—"You been up to the top?"
"Yeah, it was great!—If you go up here a bit further you'll get hailstones THIS big!" We turned round and went home for our dinner.

Look out for

"North East Wales Local Wood Directory" contains information on the history of our native woodlands, a guide to native timber and extensive info on companies based in NE Wales that supply or utilise local timber. It was produced by Coed Cymru in partnership with Cadwyn Clwyd, with assistance from Northern Marches Cymru, the Forestry Commission, WDA and local authorities. Copies available from Coed Cymru on 01824 708265 or 01352 703261. Planning Dept., Trem Clwyd, Canol y Dre, Ruthin LL15 1QA

WoodFest—woodcraft to buy as well as advice on using your own woodland; every June at St. Asaph; see www.woodfest.co.uk or Telephone: 01745 585929

Peter Boyd, woodcarver; tel; 01248 602102

Walking along the Clywedog River, near Wrexham a few weeks ago, on a high level footpath, we looked down through sparse golden coins of leaves still left clinging to spindly trees—they seemed to have their own luminescence. The buxom, voluptuous river rushed below us, 'flobbelop, slobelop, flubbelop' water brownish, greyish with white fringes where it suddenly flips up over a rock or stone and magically sprays a transparent sheet. Round the bend, over the rocks, past the eddy with capuccino foam, round, over, past and under the roots of a huge spreading tree, where otters might once have dug their tunnels up, following the roots' path in the muddy brown dark. 'Flobelop, slobelop, slopalot', rippling the gravel and sliding over the rock, nothing stops the river's force.

Steep banks above us; soil washed out from roots arching down as if scrabbling for their falling trousers of fine black slumping soil. Here, look close, tiny mosses and lichens grow—the green even more heightened in the gloom—luminous, iridescent little flakes. There is one type of moss that lives in dark cavities and uses a drop of water caught in its leaflets as a lens to magnify any scrap of light entering its hiding place.

Overlapping layers of golden, red and brown leaves all over the ground now, give the same tidying up appearance as snow, but this carpet has a golden dappling when the sun breaks through; a warming, spreading glow from patches on the ground that creeps, reflecting, up rocky banks and trees. Some trunks are smooth, dark and wet, like sleek black horses' necks. Some are crinkly-barked, some patched and flaking.

We were there to build an otter holt—a big enterprise! First dig a three metre square pit. Then line with two tiers of logs—Western Hemlock pines felled in the nearby wood for the purpose. Insert a three metre plastic pipe down to the river and leave an exit at the other side, in case of flood or predator. Then arrange the rooms inside, with two logs stacked and staked for walls between each. Otters need complete dark for breeding, so there must be a 'back room'. Some plywood sheets make the roof, with the soil, left over logs and tree-brash piled back on top. It took six of us six hours or more. What satisfaction though! To help our lovely otters;—smooth, silky wet brown, flobelop, slopalot, lolloping, frolicking otters. They are coming back, all along our cleaned up rivers in North-east Wales. Largely due to the banning of a particular type of insecticide spray on farmland since the 80's. Also in part due to the drop in persecution since otters were protected under the law, and through the Local Biodiversity Action Plan (LBAP), which covers many rare species of animals and plants. These are monitored by local volunteer naturalists as well as CCW, the North Wales Wildlife Trust and other agencies. They then share this data with the County Councils who draw up the LBAP. This process has been continuing since the Rio Summit of 1992.

Nearly all tributaries in NE Wales now either have resident otters or have otters passing along them. They have increased on the river Clwyd from records at 4% of sites surveyed in 1977 to 90% of the same sites in 2002.

Otters are rarely seen, being so shy of hunting Man, but recorders look for their tell-tale 'spraint' or droppings, and roadkill also provides useful records. Otters are also present on the Dee and many of its tributaries.

A real conservation success story, for once!

Look out for

The Three Rivers Project; volunteers carry out conservation work, including building artificial otter holts along many rivers in North-east Wales. If you would like to help contact bettylee_uk@yahoo.com or tel; 01244 550993

Otter Survey of Wales 2002 Report from Environment Agency Wales, for a

Members of the Three Rivers Project Building an Otter holt.

copy tel; 08459 333111 or email; enquiries@environment-agency.gov.uk
It is illegal to destroy or disturb otters or their habitats.
To find out more about the Denbighshire LBAP go to
www.denbighshire.gov.uk or tel;01824 708263

See other County Councils websites in the Appendix.

To report scarce animals seen dead at roadsides contact the Countryside
Council for Wales; tel; 01352 706600.

Nant Mill Visitor Centre, near Wrexham, has local walk guides and childrens
activities beside the Clywedog River and surrounding woods.

January

W e often have some alarming weather at this time of year. What a hailstorm at 3am.on Christmas night! It sounded as if it would break the windows and come through the roof. I had left a window open a crack, and the deluge of white peas forced their way in like a flood of alien missiles and buried a pile of books several feet away before we knew it. I was still able to sweep them up frozen twenty minutes later. "Oh, they're not as big as they get them in America" said my awoken teenage son, "there they have them the size of golf balls with goldfish inside them". Oh good. My husband and he then got into a discussion about how the goldfish got into them and whether a herring would be too big. Extreme weather watching seems to be becoming like extreme sport. I'm just hoping it doesn't presage worse things to come with global warming. The regular gales and flooding we now have each winter are known to be due to global warming—and that's why it's so essential to continue investing in alternative energy like wind farms on as big a scale as we possibly can.

The dreadful after effects of the underwater earthquake in the Indian Ocean at least can't be blamed on global warming—it happened on the edge of one of the continental plates that sometimes slip against each other. Some local residents here felt tremours on 21st. December that seemed a bit like a distant earthquake. On the BBC Wales news that evening they said it had been sonic booms due to the airforce testing a new super-sonic plane. British Aerospace in Preston confirmed that a Typhoon Eurofighter aircraft was on exercise over the Irish Sea at the time. There were reports from all over North Wales and

Merseyside like; "heard a loud rumbling noise", "felt the ground shaking", "the whole house shook quite violently" and "all the windows rattled".

And we do get earthquakes in North-east Wales sometimes, because we live in a rift valley, the same geological formation as the great African rift valley, only not quite as wide. The walls are made of the Clwydian hills on one side and the Denbigh hills on the other. Sometimes the faults slip and that's when we get earthquakes here. The last one I remember was in about 1991 and had its epicenter near Wrexham, and slight tremors were felt as far away as Rhyl. I was just looking at my midday napping babies and thinking "Oh god, what do I do?—my mum used to throw the kids under the bed during the London blitz..." when it was all over. I think it only got to less than One on the Richter scale, but it was still a bit scary.

I've just been reading "Gwen Tomos" (English translation from the original Welsh) by Daniel Owen. I had a devil of a job to find it. Daniel Owen was to North-east Wales what Dickens was to London and industrial England. His writing exposed the condition of the local people working in coal mines and living in the countryside—relying heavily on wild food and thus forever in trouble for poaching, a subject well covered in Gwen Tomos—those now concerned about the class warfare represented by the hunting debate could reflect on how poaching is now virtually an obsolete word, but when people were starving, for centuries "hunting" actually had an important use. The extraordinary thing is that although Daniel Owen is celebrated in his home town of Mold with a statue and a community centre named after him, none of his books have been in print (either in Welsh or English) for decades, you cannot find them second hand through Amazon and even the library behind his statue has none on the shelves! I only managed

Daniel Owen

to retrieve a damaged copy from their archives. Imagine if Charles Dickens—writing around the same time—were so ignored!

> From "Gwen Tomos" by Daniel Owen, 1894
> "I had always been a lover of nature and I was never happier than when tramping through the fields and woods gathering nuts, bird nesting, catching trout in the Alun, or if it were summer-time, basking in the sun watching the skylark ascending into the blue sky from the clover field and listening to its enchanting song. In those days, catching a water-hen or a water-rat, or destroying a wasp's nest, interested me much more than a general election. I could claim to know every chaffinch and warbler in the neighbourhood. I risked my life on two occasions to destroy a crow's nest."

Interesting how our attitude to wildlife has changed!

On the way home from scrub clearing on the Reserve we stopped off at the Ruthin Craft Centre car park to see a flock of rare Waxwings, flown in from Siberia and roosting in a little tree next to a larder of Hawthorn berries.

Lovely to see their fat, crested little bodies.

I do love the way at this time of year, when you turn a bend at the crest of a hill and see the fields below just filled up to the hedge-brims with foaming fog—as if someone had poured it from a giant jug. But it's difficult to find a lot of wildlife out there; if you fancy a bracing walk along the seashore at the Point of Ayr, following the footpath out to the RSPB hide, you can get a marvellous view of some of our winter wading birds.

But sometimes it's just nice at this time of year to curl up by the fire with a pile of seed catalogues and gardening books and plan what we can do to entice more wildlife into our garden this year. Wouldn't it be lovely to see a hedgehog or a badger and some butterflies this year?

My recommended planting list for the coming year would have to include Honesty, Lady's Smock, Aubretia and perennial wallflowers like 'Bowles' Mauve' for the Spring nectar so badly needed by all those insects emerging from hibernation. You may think you don't want to encourage insects, but without them you won't have predators for your pests, pollinators for your fruit or food for your birds and other wildlife. You also won't have the sheer lively pleasure of fluttering butterfly wings or the soothing hum of bees on a hot afternoon.

Summer-flowering plants must include Bird's-foot Trefoil, Scabious and Hebes and lots of the daisy family.

And for Autumn you really need Buddleia, Teasel, Ice plant and Hemp Agrimony.

Now it's getting towards your last chance for putting up nest boxes, planting trees and dredging ponds before things start coming to life again—the frogs and newts can start moving back into ponds to breed as early as mid February if the weather is mild. We are particularly blessed in just this part of the UK for our abundance of the rare and legally protected Great Crested Newt. We also have the other only two species of native newt—

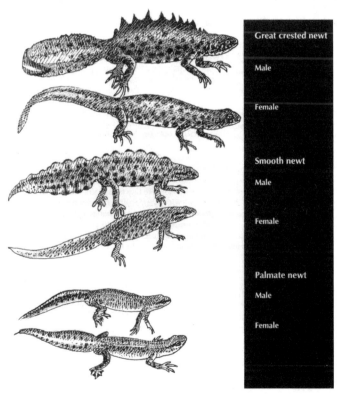

Illustration by Peter Snow from CCW booklet

Smooth and Palmate. The Great Crested in particular seems to like a network of small ponds a short distance apart, so if you make a small garden pond in this area you are more than likely to find them in it soon. Only dredge out half a pond at a time so that anything hibernating in the mud has a chance to still survive. And you don't want to have fish or ducks (they eat huge quantities of larvae in a pond) if you want wildlife like Dragonflies to live there. If you'd like to plant a wildlife hedge, or some trees for wildlife, please include Goat Willow for many moth caterpillars to feed on and Buckthorn (Alder Buckthorn, *Frangula alnus*, for damp, acid soils or Purging Buckthorn *Rhamnus catharticus*, for lime soils.) for the Brimstone butterfly caterpillars. We had a young man laying a hedge for us in January—I never fail to be fascinated by this skilled craft—if I cut any of my garden shrubs so close to the bone they would surely die. Very sharp tools and unswerving confidence seem to be the trick—you could say that applies to a lot of things in life, I suppose?

Look out for

Froglife, Mansion House, Halesworth, Suffolk IP19 8AY tel; 01986 873733 www.froglife.org, publish an excellent booklet on Great Crested Newts and wildlife ponds. CCW also has a wealth of information.(see appendix)

Buckthorn and many other wildlife plants and Lectures on gardening for butterflies; tel 01352 711198 or see **www.northwalesbutterflies.org**

Courses on Hedge-laying—Llysfasi Agricultural College: 01978 790263 admin@llysfasi.ac.uk

Advice on Hedge-laying , pond-dredging and courses on Great Crested Newts; NEWW (formerly Deeside Urban Wildlife Group), e-mail; weo@duwg.org.uk Telephone; 01244 541005

Seeds—LANDLIFE, National Wildflower Centre, Liverpool; **www.landlife.org.uk** Telephone: 0151 737 1819 Fax: 0151 737 1820

Books; "Make a Wildlife Garden" by Chris Baines and "Chris Packham's Back Garden Nature Reserve" published by the Wildlife Trusts.

Let's re-print Daniel Owen's novels! To make a request for the Flintshire Library Service to print new or facsimile editions; Community Librarian Mold Library Museum and Gallery, Earl Road, Mold, 01352 754791 email; Gillian_Fraser@flintshire.gov.uk

Gathering the Jewels website **www.gtj.org.uk**
A wonderful resource of Welsh culture and history; over 20,000 images of objects, books, letters, aerial photographs and other items from museums, libraries and record offices in Wales.

February

We had a rare treat in Denbigh with two famous performance poets visiting the town; every age group was packed to the rafters of the Town Hall to hear Benjamin Zephaniah and John Cooper Clark. My kids especially liked the latter's attempt at Haiku poetry;

> To express oneself
>   in just seventeen syllables
>   is very diffic

—and I know exactly what he means when I try to convey a message as briefly as possible on the phone or e-mail. Like when I picked up a dead Polecat on the A55 last Spring. I did so because I was hoping it might be a Pine Marten—quite a rare animal, but when inspected this one didn't have the white breast. However, I thought someone might be interested in recording this still scarce species. So I rang the Countryside Council for Wales and they were very helpful but didn't have the relevant person's phone number to hand; it was late on a Friday afternoon and they said they wouldn't be able to let me know 'til next week. "OK," I said "but what shall I do to preserve the body until then?—it's already been lying on the roadside for a couple of days and has been nibbled by something. — Shall I wrap it up and put it in the deep freeze?" They thought that was a good idea. The next week I finally got through to the woman recording polecats; "I've got this polecat in my freezer, and my family are getting a bit fed up with it—do you want it?"

"Are you sure it is a polecat? Does it have a black snout?"

"Well, it's a bit difficult to tell, you see, it's been a bit eaten..."

"WHAT?" she ejaculated "just send us the grid reference and give it a decent burial". After I'd put the phone down I wondered why she had sounded so surprised—oh no, surely she hadn't thought...?

Oh well, I often seem to say the wrong thing to people. I think that's why I like to lose myself in watching nature—it absorbs me in the complete consciousness of here-and-now and takes my mind off worrying about what I said or did in the past—or might do in the future—and it doesn't demand anything of me, it just *is*.

Lots of seed-sowing to get on with now to have those plants for wildlife I mentioned last month, but what to do about those wretched slugs that eat them off before you can blink? Slug pellets are harmful to other wildlife—I've tried just about everything else on the market, but I find the most effective thing of all is a bit of beer mixed with water in a jar sunk into the ground. Leave the rim protruding above the soil for about an inch—then the ground beetles (that eat slugs, so are your friends) don't fall in. It's such a promising time of year now, isn't it? As Benjamin Zephaniah says;

> My garden is a lively place
> There's always something happening,
> There's this constant search for food
> And then there's all that flowering,

Look out for

Animals coming out of hibernation now, but killed on the roadside, like Otters, Polecats or Pine Martens provide valuable records; inform CCW tel;01352 706600 NB.for your own safety they advise against retrieving anything from the central reservation of dual carriageways or motorways.

Special literary guest events are arranged by Denbighshire Library Service; tel;

01824 708200 . **www.cyberspike.com/clarke** for John Cooper Clarke's work and **www.benjaminzephaniah.com** for Benjamin's.

"Out and About" -each year a programme of guided walks in Denbighshire is available free from Loggerheads Country Park, tel 01352 810614, or see **www.denbighshire.gov.uk** for both these services.

In 1885 Daniel Owen wrote: "I have frequently stopped to pity the river Alun at the point where it loses itself in the Dee. From Llanarmon-yn-Ial down to Cilcain, through the Belan, along the vale of Mold, how brave and bright and beautiful it looks! But on nearing Holt its face changes, the sorrow being plainly depicted upon it of its impending absorption by the Dee." And thus it still flows, marking our border with England, full in its muddy middle-age, around the dark red sandstone castle at Holt, not far from Bangor-on-Dee so infamously flooded in 2001. No doubt there has been more flooding since as there's a large pool at the foot of the castle that wasn't there a few years ago. It is probably filling a depression where once there was a moat that accepted seasonal fluctuations of the river, the castle itself built on a high, dark purple-red sandstone outcrop so that its lower floors would have been held high up out of any flood's way.

There's not much of the castle left now—stone was robbed from it to build Eaton Hall (and probably other local buildings) once it fell out of use centuries ago. Just the Keep remains, now in danger of collapse through tree roots prising between the stonework. But, as you turn around the far side, there is a magic little hidden vista through an arched window up some worn, winding stone steps. You can suddenly hear the bustle of servants taking water for washing, or food perhaps, up this narrow passage, squeezing past each other, dropping things, cursing. The squawk of a chicken in the yard that I tripped over—but no, it was a clump of grass that brought me back to the present as my gaze was drawn upwards along the gorgeous dark red,

Cross bedding in the sandstone of the Cheshire/Wales border.

cross-bedded stone. But I just got a tantalising glimpse of what it might have been like.

You can see a lot of cross-bedding in Holt—at the Church and down on the ancient bridge that still takes the road out of town. Look for sweeping lines of slightly different colours in the stone face. Some cut across the others—caused by a change in current direction when the sand was laid down under water, or by wind. This Sandstone you can find all along the Cheshire-Wales border was laid down in the Permo–Triassic period, between about 280 to 220 million years ago, when the Cheshire basin sank and was alternately criss-crossed by river deltas depositing sediment washed down from the Welsh mountains, and then dried out and windblown in a hot desert. You can tell when sandstone has been lain down under water, rather than by wind, by looking for flecks of smooth mud in the cross-bedding.

✳

One of the less well-known wild flowers to look out for this month- what's in flower in January and February? Well, not much, but there is Gorse. You might never have looked at it very closely, thinking it a nasty, spikey, scrubby thing. But it is very unusual in this climate for being able to flower all year round. This makes it an invaluable nectar source for many insects that may venture out in a mild spell, and hence for the birds, bats and small mammals that feed on insects. It is even a larval foodplant for some butterflies. Gorse is a member of the pea and bean family (the Legumes) and the tell-tale sign is the shape of the bright yellow flowers—just like a small sweet-pea. Walking between two banks of them on a sunny winter's day you will be transported to exotic places because the scent is just like freshly-opened coconuts.

Look out for

Find Holt castle by following the footpath sign down a short, slightly sloping path from the centre of the village. More information at;
www.wrexham.gov.uk/english/heritage/holt_castle.htm

www.britannia.com/wales lots of info. incl Welsh history, literature, places to visit and all things cultural
http://www.cpat.org.ukClwyd/PowysArchaeologicalTrust

"Rhys Lewis, minister of Bethel" by Daniel Owen

www.bgs.ac.uk website of the British Geological Survey has all kinds of general interest information about rocks.

Botanical Society of the British Isles for information about our wild flowers, field trips, courses, an online identification key and lots more see
www.bsbi.org.uk or write to Mr R. Gwynn Ellis, 41 Marlborough Road, Roath, Cardiff, CF23 5BU.

TheBSBI Botanical Recorder for Denbighshire is Dr. Jean Green, tel;01745 730254 or e-mail; jean@coedduon.fsworld.co.uk

March

Now things are really beginning to warm up we will start to see insects coming out of hibernation. I am often asked for help with the identification of butterflies, and it's really important for the conservation of these rapidly decreasing creatures if you can send records of the ones you see in to 'Butterfly Conservation', the national charity that is trying to save them. But first you need to be reasonably sure you can recognise them. To begin you have to know there are only 36 different ones you will see in North Wales, and less than half of those in your garden or on walks unless you are very lucky to discover a rare colony.

And you need a book that only has British species—otherwise you spend all your time getting confused while wading through pages of similar-looking species that you're never going to see in this country anyway. A good ID book is available from Butterfly Conservation (details below).

The butterflies you can see locally can be grouped into just 7 types, of which we have; 5 colourful 'Vanessids', 5 whites, 7 Browns, 3 'Skippers', 2 Blues and 3 'Hairstreaks', some of which you may see in your garden. In addition there are 4 Fritillaries, 1 Blue, 1 Brown and 1 Skipper that are so rare there are only a few known places where they still exist. That's all you have to learn, and most of them are so distinctive that you'll very soon get to know them even when they're flying fast.

This month we will look at just the four most common and most colourful ones you can see in your garden in this area now. They are all Vanessids. Three of these are true natives—the Small Tortoiseshell with black and yellow alternate bands or squares at

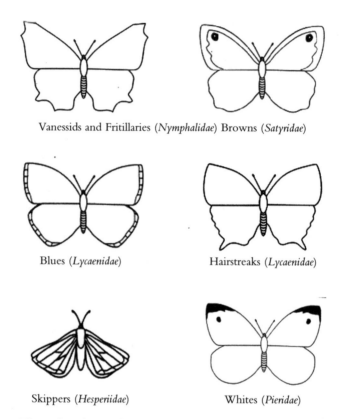

Vanessids and Fritillaries (*Nymphalidae*) Browns (*Satyridae*)

Blues (*Lycaenidae*)   Hairstreaks (*Lycaenidae*)

Skippers (*Hesperiidae*)   Whites (*Pieridae*)

The outline shapes of the six families of North Wales Butterflies.

the top edge of the wing, orange wing below, and the Peacock—our only butterfly with four distinct mock 'eyes' of big circles at the top point of its wings. (You might also see a Comma with a distinctly wiggly outline, but probably not 'til later). The other two are Red Admiral with his dramatic black jacket and white epaulettes, and the Painted Lady with lots of pale orangey brown and pink spots. These last two are immigrants each year from the warmer continent and used not to survive the winter here; but with global warming they are starting to do so. All these butterflies will lay their eggs on stinging nettles, which the caterpillars feed up on during May and June. They are our only species that eat nettles. If you cut your nettles down after the end of June, when the new growth comes through it will be just in time for the first generation of adults to lay the next brood of eggs, so you will get another batch of Vanessids.

Next month we will look at the Whites, and one or two others you can see at that time—just as different plants put on their flowers only at certain times of year, not all butterfly adults fly in the same months. And they do need it warm and not too windy before they can fly.

Is March going to go out like a lamb this year? T.H. Parry-Williams wrote;

> "Winds are necessary. Times wouldn't be there
> Without you had winds coming from somewhere."

Recently the Woodland Trust and BBC ran a project called "Spring Watch" They asked people to send in their first sightings of six key things; frogspawn, 7-spot Ladybird, Bumblebee, Peacock (the butterfly not the bird!), Hawthorn flowers and Swifts. The idea was to get a picture from the whole country of how much earlier Spring is happening now. The Springwatch interim report seemed to show that insects and plants are responding earlier to Spring than migrating birds, which means there's not so much food for their babies at the critical time. Some resident birds, however, like Herons, Song Thrush and Blackbird, (admittedly right down South), are producing chicks as early as January! Just enough time left now to put up your nest boxes— for Bumblebees that are becoming very scarce as well as for birds!

Bumblebees are enormously important for crop pollination in Britain; but now 25% of our 254 Bee species are in the Red Data Book of endangered species. This includes five species of Bumblebee that were common in the 1980s.

Bumblebees need undisturbed banks for their nests and flowers for nectar and pollen. The only six species still common are:

> Buff-tailed (*Bombus terrestris*), Common Red-tailed (*Bombus lapidarious*), Early Bumblebee (*Bombus pratorum*), Common Garden Bumblebee (*Bombus hortorum*), Common Carder or Pasture Bumblebee (*Bombus pascuorum*), and Common White-tailed Bumblebee (*Bombus lucorum*)

Bees, especially Bumblebees, need high sugar and pollen sources which have disappeared from our fields. Bumblebees also need nest sites—often vacated mouseholes in hedge banks or walls. Apparently they find these by following the smell of the mouse's urine trail (mice have weak bladders), so a good way to get them to nest in your Bumblebee nest box is to put in the entrance some old mouse bedding (either from a pet cage or bit of cotton wool previously stuffed into a house mousehole).

The high protein content in the pollen of Bird's-foot Trefoil and Red clover is important for survival of bee colonies as Bumblebee larvae feed on stored pollen.

The desperate decline of the Bumble Bee, and other bees, in our countryside is due to similar problems as for other insects, (and hence the birds and other animals that feed on them),—loss of their food and homes amongst our wild flowers and grasses on farmland and road verges that are cut too soon. The RSPB ran a survey of insects splatted on cars one summer—made fun of in the media, but there is a serious bit of research behind this.

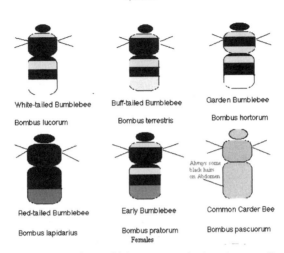

White-tailed Bumblebee
Bombus lucorum

Buff-tailed Bumblebee
Bombus terrestris

Garden Bumblebee
Bombus hortorum

Red-tailed Bumblebee
Bombus lapidarius

Early Bumblebee
Bombus pratorum
Females

Always some black hairs on Abdomen

Common Carder Bee
Bombus pascuorum

The six common British Bumblebees—upper body stripes are all yellow (narrow) and black(broader), 'tails' are of the colour as named, the Common Carder is all yellow. (with thanks to Carl Clee of Liverpool Museum) (similar charts are downloadable in colour from the Natural History museum website—see appendix)

My favourite flower this month is the Colt's-Foot—a dear little yellow daisy on a 3-inch chunky stem before its leaves, and as it ages it tends to bend over at its neck to show overlapping scales with the finest white hairs—rather like a foal's hoof with the fringing hairs around it. Along with the ubiquitous Dandelion, this is one of the earliest nectar sources for those Butterflies and Bumblebees you're now looking out for. All those Daffodils and Tulips are not much good at all!

Look out for

"Britain's Butterflies" by Still and Tomlinson, many photos from different angles plus all their caterpillars, pupae and eggs, £15 from bookshops or £12.50 from info@northwalesbutterflies.org.uk as well as a complete online Butterfly ID workshop at **www.northwalesbutterflies.org.uk** plus details of courses and walks to see rare butterflies and moths. or tel; 01352 711198. Also available; Field Studies Council Butterfly Identification chart (much lighter to carry than a book)

Recording forms for the butterflies you see are available from this website, or from Rob Whitehead, County Recorder, to whom please also send any records; Haulfryn, Graigfechan, Ruthin LL15 2HA, tel; 01824 704507

Alana Ecology sells all kinds of bird and insect nest boxes; Tel: 01588 630173 or **www.alanaecology.com**

Agralan Ltd. have wooden Bumblebee nestboxes—see Appendix.

April

This is the month when the insects are really waking up, so I want to continue my simple guide to the identification of butterflies to enable you to recognise and record the ones you see. This month we will look at just four more common ones, in the White family—sometimes called "cabbage whites" but only two of them feed on garden brassicas and nasturtium—they are the Large and Small Whites. The Large White is obviously bigger, and consequently has a more slow, gliding flight, but the two are very similar, especially if you don't see them together; pale yellow underneath, black spots on top. The distinguishing feature is that the black edging on the top wing of the Large White goes round the corner and down the edge more than on the Small White.

By comparison the other whites—Orange Tip and Green-veined White, are easy. But only the male Orange Tip has orange on his upper wings, so you might confuse the female with other whites. The underside is a dead giveaway though—all Orange Tips have a mottled green and white pattern on their lower underwing. And the Green-veined-White has yellowish or green strong ribbed veins on the lower underwing. They love to come to Honesty and Lady's Smock or Cuckoo Flower.

The gorgeous butter-yellow (where we may get the word 'butter-fly' from) Brimstone is the last species in this family that we may occasionally get in North Wales. Common in Southern England and Cheshire, they are very scarce here, thought simply because historically their only larval foodplants—the Alder Buckthorn and alarmingly named 'Purging' Buckthorn—were not used as hedging plants in this region. However, unusually for native species, the Brimstone will fly for up to 15 miles to seek out one of these small trees to lay its eggs on, so if we could all plant just one in our garden we might draw these magnificent creatures over the border from England.

You might also see one of the only three blue butterflies in this area this month—the Holly Blue, flies high up above head height, pale blue underwing with fine black dots—please let the local butterfly Recorder know if you see one, they have become scarce in recent years and we need records to try and find where they are and save them.

My favourite wildflower of this month is the extraordinary little 'Moschatel', or Mwsglys in Welsh—apparently from its musky smell. You can find this in woods and hedge banks at this time of year, forming a mat of pretty miniature aquilegia-like leaves with green flowers on two-inch stems carried above the leaves. You'll have to get down on hands and knees to see it properly, but it's well worth the effort. Completely unique in its own family, the flower of this strange plant is actually a cube formed of 5 square flowers arranged edge-on to each other. The folk name for it is 'Town Hall Clock', and you can see why.

I planted up some school wildlife gardens on Anglesey this month. One of them had a beautiful setting between three small mountains that I was told were the inspiration for the Plaid Cymru logo. One of these hills was at the edge of Parys Mountain—in the eighteenth century the biggest copper mine in the world. You could just see the old pump tower on the top of the orange scraped earth. The little children were great, as ever. These were six and seven year olds, chattering away in Welsh to me as well as their teachers—I had to stop them; "I'm sorry, I don't understand much Welsh—can you tell me what she's saying?" and there was this six year old, who couldn't read yet, translating for me as fluently in English as in his mother-tongue. I felt quite ashamed. I have lived in Wales for nearly twenty years, but east of the Conwy valley where I live, although there are plenty of Welsh speakers, it is not such a pervasive part of life as it is west of the Conwy.

We planted Red Campion, wall flowers and Honesty for spring nectar, Bird's-foot Trefoil, Hebes and Feverfew for summer and Buddleia and Hemp Agrimony for the autumn when they return to school. Funny how many kids don't know you have to take the plant out of the pot before you plant it. And they are scared of worms! They also had a pond where we planted some native weeds for newts and frogs. The Biodiveristy officer of the council had also arranged for a hedge of Hazel to be planted—there are rare native Red Squirrels on Anglesey. Red Squirrels were still to be found in Newborough forest during the early 1990s. Unfortunately, the population declined as Grey squirrel numbers increased, and by 1996 the Red squirrel was extinct at this site. Following the removal of several hundred Grey squirrels, Red squirrels were re-introduced in 2004 and have successfully bred since then.

However, the Countryside Council for Wales had wanted to remove some parts of woodland in order to recreate the open sand dune habitat that existed prior to the forest being established. What is good for sand dune species is obviously not good for Red Squirrels. Different interest groups are hoping to find a balance that accommodates all conservation objectives. The Anglesey population of Red Squirrels is now the second largest in Wales, and is the only one that exists without Grey Squirrels. Being an island it is easier to run this sort of species isolation programme on Anglesey.

Look out for
The Friends of Anglesey Red Squirrels
Llys Goferydd
Bryn Cefni Industrial estate
Llangefni, Anglesey LL77 7XA
www.redsquirrels.info/main.html

Elm is alive and well and living somewhere near you!

I went on a guided walk around a local country park about 10 years ago and was stunned speechless when the Ranger—in his late twenties—pointed out a Wych Elm to us, at the same time saying that he was not old enough to have ever seen a mature English Elm as they were wiped out by Dutch Elm disease in the mid-seventies. Good grief! A whole adult generation is now walking around, making grown-up decisions, who not only were born after Man landed on the moon, never understood what the Hippies were about, but who also have never seen—and whose grandchildren will not even see—those towering 200year old trees that darkened the lanes of Somerset when I was a child in the 60's. (I'm sure every generation has it's comparable historical landmarks, but these three are mine, and precious to me!)

I recently gave a Butterfly Identification workshop where I showed branches of Wych Elm *Ulmus glabra*, Hazel *Corylus avellana* and Old English Elm *Ulmus procera* from my own fields in Flintshire, to help people distinguish between these when looking for White-letter Hairstreak butterflies. Yes, the Old English Elm is making a come-back. But of course it has not grown into big trees yet—it is regenerating from 'dead' stumps all along our hedgerows. One attendee asked me to later go and look at her hedges—she had been told by a local County Ecologist that they were Wych Elm—they were not when I saw them—they were Old English; how old was this ecologist?— Oh, late twenties, early 30s...

So here is my simple guide to recognising these three species— not easily confused when you know what to look for.

The defining thing about all elms is that their leaves are asymmetrical; that is one side of the leaf comes further down the leaf-stalk than the other. Both Wych and Old English leaves are rough to the touch—like coarse sandpaper, but Wych Elm leaves are much bigger (3 or 4 times the size) and Wych has smooth

Old English Elm
Ulmus procera

Hazel
Corylus avellana

Wych Elm
Ulmus glabra

bark where older Old English bark is very humpy and knobbly. This latter characteristic is said to be why *U.procera* succumbed to the beetle that spread the disease, when *U.glabra* didn't, as the beetle likes to burrow into the corky ridges of the bark.

Hazel, for which elm can easily be mistaken on a casual walk along a hedgerow, has symmetrical, almost completely round leaves, and does tend to be a more light, grass-green in colour. Of course, if you see these trees in flower or fruit the difference will be quite obvious, but that will only be for a short time each year.

The new Old English Elms regenerating from suckers seem to mostly succumb to the disease again after about 20 years. This is said to be because that is when the trunk bark becomes knobbly and furrowed enough to attract the beetle. A lot of people seem to think this means there is no point in planting this species anymore, and you will not find many nurseries in the whole country that has them for sale. However I disagree; if we keep planting them then we keep the species alive and part of the gene pool; the length of time the individual trees live does not matter.

Unless, as some suggest, species like the White-letter Hairstreak can only live on the mature trees.

Research has been going on for some years to find a species of elm that is resistant to the Dutch Elm Disease. A paper has just been published on the Butterfly Conservation Hampshire Branch website entitled "The adaptation of the White-letter Hairstreak to disease-resistant hybrid and exotic elms" by Andrew Brookes. It includes information about a recently started long term study of several species of different elms planted in different locations in the county. It also contains details of suppliers of these different disease-resistant trees. You can view this paper at;
http://bchantsandiow.users.btopenworld.com/Elm_Report.htm

More information

Max Coleman at Reading University (who identified my local specimens as *U.procera*) is also researching Elm, see his paper in "British Wildlife" vol 13, no.6 August 2002 "Identification; British Elms"

He is interested in any reports of locations of existing *U.procera*, especially mature trees. E-mail him at; m.coleman@reading.ac.uk

A very limited number of *Ulmus procera* propagated from local suckers can be found for sale, as well as other butterfly and moth plants, to benefit the Butterfly Conservation North Wales Branch funds at **www.northwalesbutterflies.org.uk** or direct from; tel 01352 711198.

The Cheshire Branch of Butterfly Conservation ran a wacky and fabulously inspired project one summer when they hired an open-topped bus and parked it for a week next to an elm tree in Halton and invited people to come and see White-letter Hairstreaks from the top of it! You can see a short movie of this on their website at; **www.butterfly-conservation.com**

A nationwide project is being run by the Natural History Museum to locate remaining mature Old English Elms (*Ulmus procera*) plus using local naturalists for all kinds of recording programmes—contact them at **www.nhm.ac.uk**/science/biodiversity/index.html

Get involved with the Elm Map walks via the Ramblers' Association website or phone; 020 7339 8500.

May

The hedges are fuzzing up with green now and have been sprinkled with the little white flowers of Blackthorn for some weeks. Although these look similar to Hawthorn flowers, the Blackthorn unlike the Hawthorn, flowers on the bare wood before the leaves. Soon the more voluptuous fragrant white bouquets scattered across all our hedgerows will be Hawthorn flowers, that in folk lore are named "The May". Stop and look carefully at one of the little bunches and you will see why one of our greatest nature poets, John Clare, describes them thus:

> "There May-blooms with its little threads
> Still comes upon the thorny bowers
> And ne'er forgets those pinky threads
> Like Fairy pins amid the flowers."

The May flower was always associated with country superstition—perhaps because it flowers on May Day, traditionally the first day of Summer, and marking this time was important to ancient people to somehow bribe the gods to provide a good growing season and harvest. The carrying of a whole branch of a Hawthorn tree in flower is still part of the Cadi Ha celebration unique to the North-east corner of Wales.

Other folk traditions surrounding the May flowers include some in the south of England where it was said to be unlucky to bring the May into the house, and a child from near Ruthin told me that it is called "Mother's Death" in her family—the superstition being that if you picked it someone in your family would die. Some people remember eating the screwed up flowers on the way to school, calling it 'bread and cheese'.

"Cadi Ha"—North-east Wales' special version of May Day

On the first Saturday in May a strange group of characters will gather in Holywell High Street in Flintshire. There will be a man dressed as a woman, a blacked-face clown in a top hat and tails, a man carrying a huge branch of a Hawthorn tree and lots of children in different versions of traditional nineteenth century Welsh costume. We are familiar with many symbols left over from the pagan celebration of Spring at Mayday, but these in Flintshire are unique, even in Wales. Here it is called "Cadi Ha" and centres around the "Cadi"—the man dressed as a woman. He is supposed to represent purity and fruitfulness. He is accompanied by his Fool called Billi who carries a ladle or a frying pan in which to collect money from the crowd. Sometimes one of them used to have a broom to brush away bad spirits. The blacked faces of them and many of the dancers are also supposed to be so that the bad spirits won't recognise them and punish them afterwards!

Another important character in the procession is the Branch Bearer, who is probably the equivalent of the Green Man found in many other cultures' fertility and start-of-crop-season rituals. He walks behind the Cadi but leads the dancers and is the only one who never blackens his face. The night before Mayday he goes to cut a branch of Hawthorn—preferably in flower, but sometimes Birch or other trees have been used. He decorates the branch with coloured ribbons and silver items. This obviously has parallels with the May poles, and garlanded sticks of May celebrations in other parts of the country, but what did it symbolise? Perhaps the re-incarnation of life after the apparent death of winter—perhaps all these poles were some kind of phallic symbol representing or invoking the fertility of the earth as well?

Sometimes a person dressed as an animal is involved with the procession—the "Mari Lwyd" was a popular scare—a bleached horse's scull held aloft on a pole from which flowed a sheet covering the bearer. This local version of the Hobby Horse would chase people and even burst into houses, but seems to have been more associated with Twelfth Night and Christmas than with Mayday.

"Hwp! Ha wen!" goes the Cadi Ha song that accompanies the musicians and dancers who traditionally had to compete in how high they could jump and how loud they could screech. This has echoes of the ancient Anglo-saxon custom of 'Beltane' where the dancers had to jump as high as they could over a fire —that being how high the crops would grow. They also had to shout to scare away the evil spirits who might blight the crop.

> "Hwp! Ha wen! Cadi Ha, Morys stowt,
> (Hoop! Ha wen! Summer dance, Morris stout)
>
> Am yr uch-la 'neid-io, Hwp, dyn-a fo!
> (For the highest leaping, Hoop, that will do!)
>
> A chyn-ffon buwch a chynffon llo,
> (And tail of cow and tail of calf)
>
> A chyn-ffon Rhis-iart Par-ri'r go
> (The Blacksmith Richard Par-rys too)
>
> Hwp, dyn-a fo!"

I have not been able to find out who Richard Parrys was, or what the cow and calf tails had to do with it, but who knows how many traditions have become mixed up and forgotten in the hundreds of years that these things have been passed down? There are special long-dances incorporating the Cadi and Billi, and Billi will often just scoot off down the procession and tweak and tease by-standers.

In 1825 a William Hone observed "They are all male dancers, whose clothing is entirely new from hat to shoes. The white decorated shirts, plaited in the neatest manner, are worn over the rest of their clothes." In 1870 Jane Williams wrote that they wore "white shirts and trousers with red ribbons—in dance jumped very high"—obvious similarities with the Morris dancers of England. The "Morris" is said to come from "Mary's" and have something to do with dancing for the mother of Christ—but these traditions go back way, way further than Christianity, which was very good at assimilating pagan traditions rather than trying to exterminate them. That way people adapted to and accepted the new teachings much more easily.

By the turn of the nineteenth century, out of work colliers were seen to take these traditions along the coast from Bagillt to Bangor, and down to Ruthin and Rhuddlan. But in the hard times of the Depression, Cadi Ha seems to have degraded into an excuse for begging and generally fallen out of favour by the second World War. It was briefly resurrected in the 1960s and again in the 1980s for the local eisteddfod, usually just with school children doing some dances. But in 1998 Holywell man Chris Bailey together with the Flintshire Welsh Language Initiative based in Mold, began

The Cadi and Bili

Bili with his ladle (photo J. Miller)

The Branch Bearer
(photo J. Miller)

Bili and the Cadi dance (photo J. Miller)

to develop the festival with all the old traditions that could be found associated with Cadi Ha, and it has grown every year since. Each year there have even been visiting folk-dance troupes from Belgium, the Isle of Man and other areas. The band from Flanders was called De Wowe, who brought their own Mayday traditions to show us. These included very familiar maypole dances and quite *un*familiar tricks with huge flags—sometimes thrown up in the air and sometimes held on one foot as the dancer hopped round and round in the middle of the street. There is usually also an evening Barn Dance and other associated events.

Oh how many mysteries we have lost! But how lovely that some people are preserving them—go down to Holywell, Bagillt, Flint or Caerwys on the Saturday near May 1st and support them.

(With many thanks to Dr. Prydwen Elfed-Owens, Conwy education service and Welsh Folk Dance Society Chair, who has done much research on this subject.)

Look out for

For more information contact; The Flintshire Welsh Language Initiative, Terrig House, Chester Street, Mold. tel; 01352 755614 or see; **www.welshfolkdance.org.uk**

And please let us know if you have any memories of these traditions!

Cadi Ha celebrations take place on the first Saturday in May in Holywell, Bagillt, Flint and Caerwys. More information from; The Welsh Language Initiative, Terrig House, Chester Street, Mold. tel; 01352 755614 or see; **www.welshfolkdance.org.uk**

"John Clare, Selected Poems" Everyman's Poetry ed. By R.K.R.Thornton, Orion Publishing.

Our high hedge banks and verges foam with wild flowers just now—you could not design more beautiful herbaceous borders if you tried; every colour is there, from the little stars of Red Campion, through the yellows of Greater Celandine and Dandelion (from the French "Dent-de-lion" -referring to the lion's teeth shape on the leaf sides, rather than shaggy golden-mane flowers as I used to think when a child)—blues of Bluebells and Speedwell, to the cascades of white Queen Anne's Lace strewn along our lanes. Isn't it a pleasure to enjoy these long flower borders as we drive past, and what heartbreak when we see them devastated by the Council mowers long before they pose any visibility problem! Encouragingly Flintshire County Council are getting their County Ecologist to classify all the verges in the county according to three levels of importance to local biodiversity, and plan to change the mowing regimes accordingly. Other North Wales County Councils are also looking at this issue and if enough people contact them about it we are more likely to achieve something in other areas.

Continuing our look at the butterflies you might see in the coming month—we tend to see fewer butterflies in the garden

The same lane in Flintshire two weeks apart in May.

in June because the early ones that came out of hibernation have mated, laid their eggs and died. Their caterpillar progeny are now munching away as fast as they can before turning into adult butterflies in late June and July. That's why it is so critical that the verges are not cut until they have flown away at the end of June (and also not before the wildflowers have had time to seed). Butterflies you might see in the coming month, in addition to the White family described last time, include Speckled Wood, maybe Large Skipper, Small Copper and Common Blue—the only blue one you will see in this part of the world in June unless you go to some special places to see the Silver-studded Blue, one of our rare specialities in North Wales.

On a walk on Moel Arthur with children in the Young Archaeology Club we looked for traces of the line of Iron Age hillforts that topped the Clwydians 2,500 years ago. The remnants of great ramparts are still there—my youngest son invented a shrieking-fun race of side-rolling across the bouncy heather down into the ancient ditches with his friends—oh well, whatever it takes to get kids appreciating their environment!—It has to accommodate mountain biking, scrambling, shooters and fishers as well as those poo-leaving dog walkers—we all have our own opinion about what the countryside should be conserved

Rolling in the heather on Moel Arthur

for, and the Council's Countryside Service are applying for EU funding to conserve and enhance these rare heather moorland hills in the best way for everyone. The native Black Grouse numbers are increasing and other scarce creatures find their niche here. The air was sharp and clear, the view down the vale magnificent and the sun striking low through the tapestry carpet of new lime-green and pink bilberry shoots woven amongst the dark green heather was magic. Don't we live in a wonderful place?

Look out for

Wildlife Week usually 2nd. or 3rd. week of June; events for children and adults at many places across north Wales. For info see **www.biodiversitywales.org.uk** or in welsh is **www.biodiversitywales.org.uk/cymraeg**. or telephone 01352 810614

To speak about verge mowing tel. Denbighshire Customer Services; 01824 706 555

Young Archaeologists Club and Clwydian Range project; tel Fiona Gale 01824 708262 or e-mail fiona.gale@denbighshire.gov.uk

June

Whenever I've been feeling sorry for myself as overworked and under-assisted, trips taking kids to see local nature reserves have really lifted my spirits. Young children are great enthusiasts for wildlife—even the creepy crawlies, if adults haven't put them off with their own irrational fears already.

And Natural History is sadly missing from much of the curriculum now—partly because of teachers' work load, partly because of Health and Safety fears but partly because we've all been told not to pick the wildflowers, not to disturb nests and so on. All very well-intentioned advice, but it's a shame that it means kids rarely get close up to nature now—remember how we always used to have a Nature Table in our classrooms years ago?

Well, I took three local school groups to see different limestone grassland areas—one at Cefn Mawr quarry worked by Castle Cement near Mold. I was aided by other conservation workers from CCW, the local Councils and Coed Cymru. The children were invited to see who could make the longest list of insects they'd seen—they were running around lifting rocks, looking in cracks and hollows:

"Here's one Miss!"

"Great! A Woodlouse—but how many legs has it got?"

"Loads!"

"Yes, and how many legs does an insect have?"

"....Well, it's still going on my list!"

It was horrible weather, but we had great good fun amongst the scenery that had such an influence on the poetry of Gerard Manley Hopkins when he lived here, as discussed at the Hopkins Society workshop with Margaret Drabble, a few days before:

"And the azurous hung hills are his world-wielding shoulder
Majestic—as a stallion stalwart, very-violet-sweet!"

Continuing our look at the butterflies you might see in the coming month; midsummer is the time of the browns; Large Skipper and Small Skipper are so called after their skipping, hopping flight. They are small—about the size of a 10p. piece, and hold their hind wings at a 45 degree angle from their bodies. The Large Skipper has orange blotches on its brown wings, whereas as the Small Skipper is orangey-brown all over and flies later in the month. The Meadow Brown is one of our commonest butterflies with one distinct brown and black spot on the top-most point of each forewing, whereas the Ringlet is not so common and has many rings on under-wings and upper-wings and the Speckled Wood is dark brown with many creamy white spots. All these butterflies' caterpillars have to feed on our native meadow grasses—not the Italian Rye Grass so often sown on farms. So our nature reserves try to maintain any ancient grasslands that are left, and our road verges are some of the last corridors of this habitat.

This month you could also see Small Copper and Common Blue if you're lucky, as well as some migrants from the continent like the Painted Lady and the Hummingbird Hawkmoth—in good summers some of these species are able to fly to us all the way from the Mediterranean or even from North Africa. Do they see, like Hopkins, as they fly

"...up above, what wind-walks! what lovely behaviour
Of silk-sack clouds! has wilder, wilful-wavier
Meal-drift moulded ever and melted across skies?"

I recently published a guide leaflet, together with Alan Wagstaff who also painted and drew many of the pictures in this book, to the Eyarth Rocks Reserve, near Ruthin. The Guide was launched at Llanfair DC. primary school including an activity I ran for the children looking at the larval foodplants and colouring drawings of them, then adding stickers of the butterflies to their pictures. At the end of May I also took 40 of the children (in two groups) on a field trip to the Reserve, aided by several teachers and parents. Do you know how many forms you have to fill in to take kids on a trip these days? It nearly put me off entirely; don't do this, don't do that, Health and Safety assessment. I know some of it is a good idea, but you can see why teachers are afraid to undertake the risk of being prosecuted for an accident, and field trips are just disappearing from the curriculum. Only one little girl did fall down a grike in the

Children from Llanfair Dyffryn Clwyd primary school on a field trip to Eyarth Rocks Butterfly Reserve, May 2004.

Volunteers at Eyarth Rocks Reserve in January 2005 taking a break having cleared the limestone pavement of trees growing out of the grikes.

limestone pavement, but we managed to pull her straight out so nothing was damaged. Several bare-legged children were stung by nettles, but they all seemed to have enjoyed the afternoon, seeing many Pearl-bordered Fritillaries, finding fossils and learning about the wild flowers, larval foodplants and why the Reserve is important. It was a gloriously sunny day and the Pearl-bordered Fritillaries, one of the rarest butterflies in Europe, were flying all around our ankles; "Ooh, there's another one Miss!" "Is that a rare one Miss?" "Look, look! There's a Dark Green Fritillary Miss!" "Er, no, I don't think so because it's not the time in the year for them to fly yet..." "Yes it is, Miss, because *I know*!"

The kids were just delightful. Although health and safety requirements are a concern on such visits, the pleasure and educational value for both children and adults involved is immense.

We completed the fourth winter of scrub clearance on the reserve in March 2005—by then some eight acres had been cleared by local volunteers for Butterfly Conservation, and the limestone pavement was again visible. Some scrub was left for shelter belts. The volunteer Reserve Manager, Rob Whitehead, then wanted to halt the scrub clearance for a few years to see how the butterflies respond. He reported the highest count of Pearl-bordered Fritillaries in 2005 for over twenty-five years; 98 individuals seen on one day at the peak of the flight period in late May. There had been maximums of about 100 in the 1980's, but that was over the whole hill, not just the 22 acres that is now the Reserve. In 1997 and '98 there were maximums of 45 on the adjoining land plus the Reserve area—only about 20 to 25 on the latter. But in 2004 only about seven were seen on the adjoining land, so we must be doing something right on the Reserve!

Pearl-bordered Fritillary females have been observed laying their

Eyarth Rocks Butterfly Conservation Reserve.
Inset, Pearl-bordered Fritillary.

eggs in the newly-cleared areas, and 2005 saw the return of the Dingy Skipper and Grayling, but still no sign of the Grizzled Skippers that used to be found here. However, we hope this scarce species may still be hanging on somewhere closeby and will return now its habitat is being restored.

Bracken strimming and raking-off on 100metre squares are continuing and violet regrowth is being monitored; volunteers will still be needed to help with this effort.

What a lovely mid-summer sight—Swallows swooping over the buttercup-filled meadows, a whole family of them bred in the stables and now hunting insects together. Smart dark-blue dinner suits with forked tails and white shirt-fronts. When they stop for a breather on the roof or telephone wires, you can tell the juveniles by their white lips or 'gape' left over from prompting mum to feed them in the nest. I'm relieved most of the family seems to have survived because we had to put wobbly wire netting up across most of the doorway to stop the Magpies getting in and flying up to peck down the babies from the nest. But one day I even saw a cheeky Magpie balancing on the top of the wire.

I don't mind the Magpies—it's just part of nature that they should look for an easy meal. They're beautiful too, I love the way there's a sweep of white semi-circular wing on the glossy blue-black as they take off—like I used to see the Indian Roller take off from the paddy fields in the same way—their semicircle was of turquoise blue. But I put out bread and left over chicken for the Magpies, they don't need to eat my live Swallow babies. You can soon tell when the nest is threatened, the chit-chit-chattering of the parent Swallows is intense as they dive bomb anything (including me) that comes near.

My wildflower of this month is Bird's-foot Trefoil (*Lotus corniculatus*)—so called because the seed-pods are grouped in threes or fours and go brown, looking just like a wild songbird's foot. 'Trefoil' means the leaf is divided in three—like many legumes, or pea and bean family, this one also produces its own nitrogen in nodules on its roots, and so can grow in the most infertile of places. It's often seen at the side on the road, where it doesn't mind being mowed off occasionally—in fact it enjoys the lack of competition from grasses and other vigorous plants that have been cut. The flowers, like golden yellow and orange sweet peas, tumble over rocks and walls if planted in the garden. It is the essential larval foodplant for the Common Blue and several other butterflies and moths and also provides high-protein pollen for Bumblebees, so it's a must for any wildlife garden. There is loads of it on the old coal tip workings at Talacre, growing amongst the bare gritty ground where all kinds of wild orchids also thrive. Dingy Skipper butterflies join the Common Blues and Skylarks with their clear high song. Rare species like the Natterjack Toad and Sand Lizard have recently been introduced to the Talacre area, so it's important to preserve it and not flood it to make up for dredging Mostyn Docks as has been suggested.

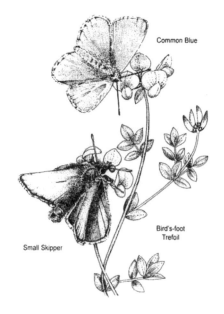

Common Blue

Bird's-foot Trefoil

Small Skipper

Line drawing by
Alan Wagstaff.

Another wildflower open just now is in frothy white flat umbrellas on the elder trees. There are a number of old country recipes for this wild free food, like fritters made by frying the battered flowers, or ice-cream syrup made by adding them to a boiled sugar solution and then frozen. But my favourite is Elderflower champagne.

Elderflower Champagne

4 large heads of elderflowers, picked on a dry,
sunny day
Juice and thinly pared rind of 1 lemon
2 Tablespoons of white vinegar
1.5 lb (700g) granulated sugar

Place all ingredients in a large container with 8 pints (4.5 litres) water. Stir to help dissolve the sugar, cover with a cloth and leave for 24 hours. Strain and pour into sterilised screw-top bottles that have previously held a sparkling drink. Screw on caps tightly and leave for two to three weeks before sampling so that it develops a fizz. Store in a cool place. Drink within three months (if you can save it for that long).

Look out for

Annual National Moth Night—lots of moth-trapping events taking place across the region—see the Events page on
website; **www.northwalesbutterflies.org.uk** or Tel 01352 711198
Bird's-foot Trefoil plants also available from this website and number.

July

Overheard at the North Wales Garden Festival at Bodelwyddan Castle recently, from amongst the public at the Badger Group stand; "Come on, I'm going to sign the petition against gassing them".

"No, I'm not signing that!—they spread TB!"

"Rubbish! That is an absolute MYTH!"

"It's not—I saw a cow giving birth once and the badger came up and ripped the bag off the calf and ate it before the cow knew what was going on!"

"Nonsense!"

"It did! I saw it myself!"

"Well, it might have done that, but it wouldn't have given it TB!"

They almost came to blows. But it made me wonder just what the evidence is, so I enquired from various sources. On the Department of Food and Rural Affairs (DEFRA) website there is a mountain of papers on the subject, but even the most recent ones say there is still no proof that Badgers spread TB to cattle, and that more long term field trials need to be done. (It is not the same type of TB as humans get).

A paper published in Nature on 26 May 2005 has found that cattle movements "substantially and consistently outweigh all other variables" for predicting the presence of bovine tuberculosis amongst cattle. Badgers, deer and other wildlife may yet be shown to play a minor role, but the current scientific evidence confirms that DEFRA's new strategy to clamp down on the movement of cattle is going to be effective in controlling bovine TB.

Anyway, I thought the main argument was that even if wild animals can and do spread disease, the culling of them in any area simply leads to more wild animals from outside flooding in to take their place—so if the disease wasn't spreading before, it sure will be then!

Arriving in North Wales and driving along the A55 near Abergele, not far past the much smaller Bodelwyddan Castle, visitors see our fabulous fairytale Gwrych Castle and its high lookout tower against the grand sweep of the wooded limestone hill. What could be our great tourist attraction, museum for local treasures (currently they all go to Cardiff), conference centre and hotel as well as indoor play wonderland for local children in winter—also with large grounds and woods that shelter much scarce wildlife—had to be dropped from the BBC "Restoration" series because the Council did not issue in time the long promised compulsory purchase order from the absentee owner. The TV programme gave the impression that Graded listing saves a building. It doesn't. Gwrych has been a Grade 1 listed building since 1996, but it has still been allowed for the roof to fall in and the great marble staircase and fireplaces to be stolen away and sold through 'reclaim' yards and websites. The whole castle is now too unsafe for visitors to go near and despite years of campaign by its Preservation Trust, the compulsory purchase order, without which no-one can act, has not materialised. Now a new business park is being built in front of it with trees that will obscure the wonderful view from the road. It seems as if the powers that be are just waiting for the castle to become too derelict and so unsafe that they will be able to let it collapse and have no more responsibility for it. What is the point of Grade 1 listing then? Do write to local Councillors and join the Trust –if

Gwrych Castle near Abergele

enough people get interested in saving this fabulous building we may yet at least have the exterior left to enhance the landscape.

As I write this in 2005 another feasibility study was being done after which it is hoped that the Council will issue the compulsory purchase order—but I'm inclined not to hold my breath!

A plant hunt at Eryrys, near Llanarmon yn Ial, with the local conservation society. Pale green gentle hills, a bit of bare limestone pavement, soon out on the top with wonderful views across the Clwydians. We found Frog orchids, Common Spotted purple orchids, Field Gentian, wild Scabious, lots of Bird's-foot Trefoil and therefore lots of Common Blue butterflies. And we also saw amongst the sheep-sheared turf, my favourite wild flower of this month, the diminutive Milkwort, *Polygala vulgaris*. Strangely I first came across this tiny little blue gem on an acid, windswept, sodden Scottish moor many years ago. But another virtually identical species also grows happily in thin-soiled dry limestone pasture. The name is said to come from its indication that where it grows is good for milk cows. But I've only ever found in very short, sparse grass! In fact generally over the countryside, the less grass there is, the more wild flowers there are—grass is such a strong competitor. And that's why, I think, limestone hills are so good for our dwindling wildflowers and the insects and birds that feed on them; simply because grass doesn't grow so strongly there. The Welsh name for Milkwort is Amlaethai cyffredin. A unique shaped flower, appearing 5-petalled, but in fact made up of three sepals and just two petals. The flower is one of the few true blues, but can also occur in pink and white.

I went this month to a Cheshire Branch of Butterfly Conservation event. They had speakers from various conservation organisations, including The National Trust. This usually brings to mind grand stately homes, but in fact it owns large areas of unspoilt countryside including 466 Sites of Special Scientific Interest (SSSI) in England and Wales, 10% of all the National Nature Reserves (NNRs) as well as having 41% of the UK Biodiversity Action Plan (BAP) species on National Trust land (NT)—lectures in conservation are always full of acronyms! Also, 80% of NT land is farmed by some 1300 tenants and graziers, most of this land currently overstocked and overgrazed because of ancient agreements. However the NT is now trying to reform this, partly by not investing in farms that don't meet their biodiversity aims. The NT is also sponsoring a lot of research on rare and endangered species of all kinds in Britain. In their report they say "Global warming is an atmospheric oil tanker; it will take a very long time to stop or to turn around. Species may find their preferred temperature range moving up to 150 Kilometres north and will have to move with it, across an intensively managed, crowded and fast changing landscape." And they set out their plans to strike a balance between their different obligations on NT owned land; for public access, to those including farmers making a living from it and to internationally agreed conservation objectives.

Iolo Williams came to interview Rob Whitehead (volunteer Reserve manager) and me for Radio Wales about Eyarth Rocks Reserve (another SSSI, but this one now owned by Butterfly Conservation). Iolo's a member and enthusiast for Butterfly

Iolo Williams, BBC Wales wildlife programme presenter with Rob
Whitehead and Jan Miller, Eyarth Rocks Reserve July 2005

Conservation too, and was very interested in our progress,
especially as Rob was able to tell him that the maximum count
of the rare Pearl-bordered Fritillaries this year was 98, after last
year's max of 65, and the four previous years' 54, 35, 17 and 4
respectively. We also told him that we now have EU Objective
One funding to fence the reserve so that limited grazing will
keep the scrub down in future.

On a golden afternoon it's a good steep, windy walk up the path
from the Jubilee Gate, south-westwards from Penmaenmawr.
Before walking over the crest and turning to look at the view you
can see Graig Lwyd half quarried away on the north side. Four
hundred feet has been taken away in the last century, totally
destroying the hill fort Brach-y-Dinas, with little recording. On

the geological map this mountain stands out as a red blob—about 400 million years ago in the Ordovician period it was a magma chamber—where molten lava collects before erupting out the vent of a volcano. This whole area, including parts of Snowdonia, was a scene of intense volcanic activity during that period. This magma chamber would have been several kilometres underground and when the volcanic activity ceased it would have cooled very slowly over thousands of years. Its outside edges would have cooled fastest resulting in a very fine grained rock—in this case almost a glass with a distinctive conchoidal fracture, that is, a shell-like concave break with radial patterns. Such rock gives a very sharp knife edge and was of course exactly what Neolithic man was looking for. He must have known his environment intimately to have been able to find this rock formation (by then uplifted and eroded) thousands of years before geologists gave it the name micro-tonalite or micro-diorite.

There is a wonderful view across the Menai Straights and out into the Irish Sea, with the Great Orme and Puffin Island punctuating the glistening sea. With the recent excavations of the Iron Age copper mines on the Great Orme it has been confirmed that this area was a hive of industrial activity in prehistoric times. Evidence that the stone axes from Penmaenmawr were traded far afield is found in forty places around Wales and southern England. These Graig Lwyd axes have been found from Anglesey to Wiltshire and Cambridgeshire. Their distribution gives an idea of a trade which carried them coastwise and southward. Copper was being won from the Great Orme mines as long ago as 2000 BC—the same period as Graig lwyd axes were being manufactured as 'roughs' on the slopes of this mountain and transported to other places to be finished off. Great Orme copper was traded with Ireland and further afield, so that this area has been described as the 'Sheffield of the Stone Age'. There was probably an overlap into the Bronze Age too—stone axes continued to be used by ordinary people.

The last Ice Age ended some 10,000 years ago, the climate warmed up and Man moved in. The landscape would have been tundra with oak, elm and elder forest and during the Neolithic period it was two or three degrees warmer than today and there was a thriving agricultural community up on these hills; the area is littered with stone circles, hut circles and ancient field banks. Now it is so bleak it's hard to imagine.

The Ice Age would have left plenty of bare, shattered rocks, easy for early Man to just pick up material suitable for tools. Later wooden scaffolding would have been set against the rock face and fired, to crack the larger faces of rock into more workable pieces. From the sea (as from the new coast road) you can see a large upright stone marking this locality—as if the prehistoric workers had their version of a giant McDonald's 'M' sign to guide the way for customers. The largest stone circle dates from 1450 BC, and the cremated bones of three children, between ten and thirteen years old, were found inside it. Perhaps when so many infants died young, the ones that reached this age were the most precious to sacrifice to the gods of food and weather. Smaller circles here date from 1100 to 1400 BC, and all these circles are in alignment, each with broken quartz in the centre. One theory is that they were used for night time ritual when the quartz would glow in the moonlight.

If you look at a map of all the stone and timber circles in Britain it strikes you that there was at least one for every settlement—just like there are churches in every village today.

This month we can trap quite a few moths—you can catch them at any time of year, but you get the greatest numbers in July and August. Moths, actually in the same family as butterflies, are generally not as popular,—thought of as boring brown and they bat into you in the dark. But many moths are just as beautiful as butterflies, though rarely seen because they fly at night. Moths have the most poetic names, given by the Victorian enthusiasts who first collected them—names like "Scarce Vapourer", "Rosy Footman" and "Flame Brocade" are all very descriptive; but some moths obviously frustrated their would be identifiers—"The Uncertain" and "The Confused" are names still in the reference books!

Moth-trapping involves attracting them to a funnel under a very bright lamp where they fall into a box. We identify them and then release them. There are a lot more native moths in the UK than butterflies—about 800 of the larger (or macro) moths and only 55 butterflies. This may be because moth caterpillars are less fussy about which wild plants they can eat, but still many moth species are under threat due to loss of natural habitat, and trapping them is how we record which species are present in each area so we can monitor their decline or increase.

In Downing Woods, once the estate of 18th. century naturalist Thomas Pennant, we caught delicate, palest yellow-white Swallowtail moths—so called because of the points on their large hindwings. We had Footmen—with their grey morning-coats edged in cream, pale green Emeralds with their wings spread far flat and an enormous Poplar Hawk Moth—holding its grey and rust wings out like a crinoline skirt. We were hoping to find the rare Netted Carpet Moth, known from only two localities in Britain, whose larvae feed on the nearly as rare native Yellow Balsam. This is similar to the Hymalayan Balsam—the big pink "Policeman's hats" that are a foreign invasive species taking over many of our waterways. Just like this one, the native Yellow Balsam has exploding seed pods that fire the seeds a long distance. It is these seeds that the moth caterpillar feeds on, but it has 'learnt' to bite through the ligament that fires the seed from the seed pod without triggering the mechanism. Incredible.

Amazing and beautiful as moths can be, they are of course food for a number of other creatures—especially Bats. One Pipistrelle Bat (our smallest native species) can eat 3000 insects in one night. The local Bat Group run events across the area to help the public get to know these other mysterious night creatures, also endangered due to loss of habitat. In the Greenfield Valley there are eight of the ten species we have left in North Wales. We saw large Daubenton's Bats fly low across the reservoirs at dusk—skimming the water's surface. We were given bat-detectors to hear the different ultrasonic sounds each species makes and help us to know what we can barely see in the blackness. It is amazing how you really can see something better with your eyes when you've learned to identify it beforehand.

Thomas Pennant: North Wales pioneer of natural history and travel writing

Thomas Pennant was born in 1726 and his life spanned most of the eighteenth century—a time of transition like today, though the transition he was part of was not from industrial to information age, but from agrarian to industrial and from an age of blind faith to discovery and invention.

However, unlike other movers and shakers of this great transition—Linnaeus, Banks, Captain Cook, Dr.Johnson and Gilbert White, all of whom Pennant regularly corresponded with, Pennant himself is virtually unknown. Many people know Gilbert White's "Natural History of Selbourne" as one of the first accounts of a local botany and zoology, but what they do not know is that this book was compiled from letters that White wrote to Thomas Pennant. It's such a pity that he didn't include the corresponding letters from Pennant!

Pennant himself wrote five tomes on natural history, and six travel books. These were some of the first "tourist guides" ever, championed by Dr. Johnson who said Pennant was "the best travel writer I ever read". Thus Pennant may be one of the first to have stimulated interest in the countryside. But he also described the conditions of ordinary people, as well as the wealthy, so that these are rare contemporary accounts of the Industrial Revolution's impact on social history.

The Pennant family had farmed land in the parish of Whitford, near Holywell in Flintshire, since the Norman Conquest. In the mid-fifteenth century Thomas's ancestor, David ap Tudor, took the name of 'Pennant' from the Welsh 'Pen-y-nant' meaning 'head of the valley'; they must have been a wealthy family by then to have taken a surname instead of the usual 'ap' (meaning 'son of') as had been the Welsh tradition. One early member of this family was Abbot of the monastery at Basingwerk (Holywell), but he had seven children! His illegitimate son succeeded him as Abbot and oversaw the dissolution of the monastery under Henry VIII.

Thomas Pennant's father inherited the Downing (thought to be a corruption of "Eden Owain"- the Welsh name of the area) estate in 1724 from a childless relative, which increased the wealth of the family that now rivalled the other great local family, the Mostyns. Thomas was the only son of three surviving children, and he was fostered out to a local poor family until the age of seven, as was the custom among the local gentry. Then he was sent to Wrexham Grammar School as a boarder. He seems to have been a happy child and recounts being given a book on birds at a young age that inspired his passion for ornithology, and natural history in general.

At fourteen he went to a school in Fulham, London, where he studied Greek, Latin and French, in between some bouts of serious illness. In 1744 he went to Queens College, Oxford. He seems to have got into some trouble between the Dons and the undergraduates, and the ring-leaders were sent down, but Pennant was merely transferred to Oriel College, being required to pay some "caution money".

While still an undergraduate Thomas made an excursion to Cornwall, where he gained a passion for Geology, then a very new science. He began regular correspondence with the leading international naturalists of the age, including Stillingfleet, Ellis, Da Costa and Linnaeus.

Throughout the 1750's his main interest was Geology, and he made regular fossil-hunting trips in the Welsh Borders and Snowdonia; 800 of his specimens are in the Natural History Museum in London. He also made a trip to Ireland, but writes that "such was the conviviality of the country that I found myself distracted from the original aim of collecting fossils and minerals"

You can still walk through the Downing estate; a public footpath from the end of Upper Downing Road, opposite The Huntsman pub in Whitford, takes you on a damp and muddy wander through overgrown woods, mostly unmanaged rhododendron, sycamore and conifers; but you may notice the occasional oddity of a monkey-puzzle tree, or a North-American Giant Redwood

Downing Hall and its library, in the early 20th century.

rising out of them. These were planted by Thomas Pennant as seed sent back to him by Banks, and others, when they were first discovered. So along with Kew Gardens the Downing woods must contain some of the oldest living specimens of the first plants sent to Britain by explorers. But there seems to be no preservation order on them; few people know they exist.

Local families have walked by the rushing streams and fish-ponds for hundreds of years, but now developers are buying up individual plots and trying to keep walkers out. A clearing opens out onto a rubble-strewn area where once the Great Hall stood. All that remains now is the Coach House, which is often mistaken for the main house, but that was demolished in 1953 by the council as unsafe, having been a ruin since fire destroyed a large part of it in the 1920's. Luckily there is a photograph of it before that fire.

Pennant even built a furnace in the grounds of Downing where he experimented with smelting ores and melting minerals. Huge heat and pressure is needed for many of these, so it must have been quite a dangerous occupation! By the 1760's he felt, surprisingly, that he "had completed his collection in that branch of Natural History", and began work on his "British Zoology", which was eventually published posthumously because he couldn't get his father's approval for funding the enterprise. Thomas Pennant died in 1798, having written 18 major books. In addition to writing a British Zoology, he also wrote an Indian and an Arctic Zoology, without ever having visited those continents! His information was gleaned from explorers and people who had lived there. We may find this difficult to take seriously today, but Pennant's skill was in putting together disparate bits of information and being one of the first people to try and come out with a sensible method of classification. Of course, since then, his work has been eclipsed by many others working with more accumulated knowledge, but we should not forget Thomas Pennant as one of that extraordinary breed of thinkers and explorers of knowledge without whom our understanding of the natural world would be greatly impoverished now.

(With thanks to Paul Evans and Goronwy Wynne.)

Look out for

Gwrych Castle Preservation Trust; **www.gwrychtrust.co.uk**
tel; 01745 857139 (leave message)
7 Clive Avenue, Prestatyn LL19 7BL, Denbighshire

Llanarmon yn Ial Conservation Soc. T. Rigby 01824 780408

BBC Radio Wales series "Natural Histories"
(including our interview with Iolo Williams) broadcast in the
winter of 2005.

www.nationaltrust.org.uk or
National Trust Office for Wales
Trinity Square, Llandudno LL30 2DE
Tel 01492 860123

For report; "Nature Conservation in a Living countryside"
www.naturedetectives.org.uk for news about Autumn Watch with the
Woodland trust and the BBC. Also resources in Welsh.
Graig Lwyd Neolithic Axe Factory nearest town: Conwy Nearest Village:
Penmaenmawr Map Ref: SH717749 Landranger Map Number: 115

DEFRA (used to be Ministry of Agriculture Fisheries and Food) website;
www.defra.gov.uk
Cattle movements and bovine tuberculosis in Great Britain. Gilbert
et al., *Nature* 435, 491-496; 2005. 26 May 2005. www.nature.com

Clwyd Badger Group, PO Box 708, Mold Post Office, Mold, Flintshire
CH7 2AA, tel; 01244 544823

Dates of local moth-trapping nights and pictures of local rare moths at
www.northwalesbutterflies.org.uk or telephone 01352 711198.

"Moth-er's Union" (informal moth ID meetings) are held on the first
Monday evening of each month and an annual event takes place in July to
search for the Ashworth's Rustic and Weaver's Wave moths unique to this
area at Pensychnant Conservation Centre, near Conwy, tel.01492 592595

A monthly moth group also meets at Treborth Botanical Gardens, Bangor.
As well as many local plant enthusiasts; The Friends of Treborth Botanic
Garden, University of Wales, Bangor LL57 2RQ. Tel (01248 353398)
www.treborthbotanicgarden.org
Thomas Pennant Society

A pack of guide leaflets of "Pennant Walks"and information about
The Pennant Society is available from; N. Closs-Parry, Bryn Ceris, Carmel,
 Holywell CH8 7DD   tel; 01352 711036

North Wales Bat Group; tel; 01745 540360, e-mail; mike.castle@which.net
Send moth records for Denbighshire to Bryan Formstone, 15 Beech Ave.,
Gresford, Wrexham LL12 8EL, tel 01978 855174

For Flintshire to David Bennet, Arosfa, Rhes y Cae, Flintshire CH8 8JG, tel
01352 780787

The Moth-Trap

They keep their secrets well,
Lapped in the barren folds of granite
Above the tree-line,
Feeding on vetches, thrift and creeping things.
For three decades till now we had not glimpsed them,
Up there,
High on the humming mountainside at midnight.

>Our forbears gave moths names:
>The Annulet, Small Dusty Wave, the Hebrew Character.
>Striving to catalogue and own them
>We marvel at the myriad differences,
>Yet never master them.
>When Ashworth's Rustic flies to light
>We thrill to recognise

But are ourselves the strangers.
We release them, and they fly
Back to the darkness and their hidings.

>Each year their drama is played out,
>Hatching and crawling, searching and eating, till rest comes.
>Predestined cells, miraculous,
>Dissolve, then knit to a new excellence,
>A feathery ecstasy of wings and questing tongues,
>Tuned to the sweets of nectar
>And the mate-attracting scent beyond our senses.

Those lepidopterists of yesteryear
Had no mercurial lures to cheat the dark,
No dazzling invitations in the night.
Treacle, perhaps, could tempt,
But nothing could avoid for them
The slow, painstaking search for eggs, for larvae,
The creeping evidence of life out there,
Present and future.
We in our century expect to see
Dozens each summer night.

>So, were they always there,
>The years we never saw them, Annulets?
>Living their quiet, private, secret lives,
>They never missed us.
>We really do not matter much.
>But I am swirled into their mystery.
>The chambers of my heart
>Quail with the awe of this.

Is it then such a virtue to be rare?
I am hushed with wonder that they are still there.

Alice Wakefield

90

August

Lots of butterflies on the Buddleia bushes now—but actually only about half a dozen different species in most gardens, if you look closely. You will see the dark-spots on orange-brown Comma—the only one with a wiggly, irregular outline. Then the Peacock—the only one with big circular blue 'eyespots' to fool the birds on its deep red wings. The brown and orange Gatekeeper is so called because it is often seen flying up and down a hedgerow—across gateways. It can be confused with the female Meadow Brown that also has orange blotches—but look for the double spot on the upper wing and a brown border around the edge of all the wings to tell it is a Gatekeeper. The Small Tortoiseshell has distinct black and yellow bands, (or squares like a tortoise's shell) on the top edge, whereas the Red Admiral has diagonal red and white stripes, like epaulettes on its shoulders. This one plus the Painted Lady, that we have had loads of in recent hot summers, are migrants from the continent and seem to be in short supply in other years—our local

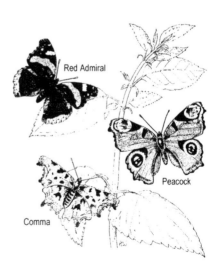

Red Admiral

Peacock

Comma

Line drawing by
Alan Wagstaff

Recorder would be interested to hear of your sightings.

Looking for Purple Hairstreak butterflies in the valley in August, we didn't quite have the weather—butterflies need sun to warm up their wing muscles—but we did see a couple—far up in the oak tree canopy, where the caterpillars feed on the leaves and the adults feed on the honeydew from aphids, like fluttering silver sweet papers from underneath. We also saw lots of Gatekeepers—orange with brown border—and a Holly Blue—much easier to spot at eye level on bramble flowers. However, Brian and Sue Roberts who monitor the butterflies in the valley, had two much more exciting encounters recently—a White-letter Hairstreak and a Clouded Yellow nectaring on big stands of fluffy pink Hemp Agrimony flowers. Both butterflies are very scarce—the former because its larval foodplant was mainly Old English Elm, so devastated by Dutch Elm disease, and the latter because it is a migrant from the warmer Mediterranean.

Unsurprisingly, my favourite wildflower for August is the Hemp Agrimony—*Eupatorium cannabinum*; so called after the Mithridates Eupator, King of Pontus, who believed in its medicinal properties and planted it everywhere. You find it mostly by rivers and ponds. It is the only member of the family native to Europe and west Asia—most of the Eupatoriums are native to the Americas, where they have the common name "Joe Pye Weed" after an Algonquin Indian who used the plant to treat Typhus. Various members of the Eupatorium family—(now sometimes called Ageratina and related to our familiar garden Ageratum) are still used in Chinese medicine. I became very interested in them because of their great attraction to butterflies. They come in huge tall forms of purple, pink and white, as well as medium and small lilac and blues and have a longer flowering season than the Buddleias and so extend the attractiveness of the garden to butterflies. I enquired about where the National Collection (NCCPG) of them was held in this country and discovered there was none, so I have started collecting and applied to the NCCPG to hold it myself. Most of my new ones are only just coming into flower as I write this, but I'm eager to see which ones will attract most butterflies.

I also have to say something in defence of Ragwort, however contentious, this month. Common Ragwort (*Senecio jacobaea*) is a valuable nectar source for hundreds of insects and is the foodplant of at least 77 species. Over two thirds of these species are very reliant on the plant, and include seven Nationally Scarce species (three beetles, one fly and three micro-moths), and three Nationally Rare (Red Data Book) ones. The most well known is the day-flying scarlet Cinnabar moth. The Cinnabar's striking black and yellow caterpillars are well known.

It is also a very important nectar plant for many species of butterflies and other insects that don't come to garden flowers. I know so many people want to eradicate Ragwort because it is poisonous to stock, but animals tend not to eat it when it is standing, (they know what is not good for them), but only when it has been cut and inadvertently mixed up with the hay. By all means let us pull it out of fields where stock graze, but please can we allow some of it to grow in waste places and by the roadside? We have lost so much of our natural biodiversity in this country, we should not be trying to eradicate any more of it.

Old Colwyn Environment Association have just (2005) won the first prize in the annual Snowdonia Wildlife Gardening competition. The project includes three butterfly-attracting gardens that I planted for them in St. John's churchyard, Wynn Gardens and Tan y Coed parks. Each garden has an interpretation board which tells you which of the plants attract which butterflies at different times of year.

Look out for

Pictures of the Colwyn Bay gardens plus their plants including Eupatoriums available from **www.northwalesbutterflies.org.uk** or tel 01352 711198.

Ragwort info—see appendix.

A Brief History of the Greenfield Valley

The Greenfield Valley in Holywell has been an important site for hundreds of years because of the natural Vauclusian spring that emerges from underground where the limestone of the hill above meets a layer of impervious clay. This sudden appearance of water from 'nowhere' probably gave rise to the legend surrounding the 'Holy Well' and Saint Winefrid (Gwenffrewi in Welsh). She was a religious young woman who resisted the advances of the wicked chieftain Caradoc, who in fury cut off her head with his sword. Where her head hit the ground the magical spring of water appeared and Gwenffrewi's uncle, St. Beuno, picked up the severed head and stuck it back on. The restored virgin entered a nunnery and lived a saintly life til an old age. There are several statues and paintings of her in the area that show the scar around her neck. How this became translated in the Middle Ages to being the special shrine for women to attain fertility after years of barren marriage is unclear. Nowadays coaches of pilgrims still come to immerse themselves in the healing waters and the local Council has put up a brown tourist sign as you enter Holywell saying "The Lourdes of Wales".

In the Mediaeval period the Earl of Chester's castle was built to protect the holy well, and Basingwerk Abbey was founded nearby because of it. Holywell became a Jesuit centre for all North Wales and a large part of Cheshire. By the time the Industrial Revolution started, the Feast of Saint Winefrid would attract 2000 people, and it was a famous site of pilgrimage. So when Lancashire industrialists were looking for steep river valleys on which to build more water mills, Holywell was an obvious site—Cheshire was too flat. The first mills were built here for copper working; begining in 1743, there being six copper mills by 1780. The first cotton mills arrived in 1787, one started by Arkwright of water-frame fame, who was looking for a new site after an argument with his partner Smalley. There followed a woollen mill and lead smelting works. With coal on the coast at the bottom of the valley, the whole area became a very important industrial centre. The census of 1851 shows the population of Holywell was 10,000, with 2,500 to 3000 living just in the High Street area. This meant Holywell was the third largest town in Wales; only Swansea and Merthyr were bigger at that time. As a result Holywell was one of the first places to get its own Gas Works, in the 1820's.

A Tramway used to cross the road on a trestle bridge near the holy well. Horse-drawn trams pulled minerals up the valley before the railway was built. A special limestone was mined nearby called locally 'Aberdo'(a corruption of Abertawe from the South Wales site). A cement could be made from this limestone that would harden underwater, and was used to build a great part of Liverpool docks. It was just a one and a half hour journey by boat to Liverpool from Greenfield Dock, and this meant Greenfield was an important corner of the triangle of shipping trade in the 18th. century. Ships came here from Liverpool bringing raw materials and left carrying copper goods made in the valley from Anglesey's Parys Mountain copper ore, to trade on the West coast of Africa for slaves. Slaves were then taken to the USA or Carribean, and cotton or sugar brought on the last leg of the triangle back to Liverpool. Thus the slave trade has been an important factor in the prosperity of most of the wealthy families of North Wales.

The copper-beating, or "battery", works in the Greenfield Valley also produced copper sheeting to clad the hulls of ships sailing to tropical waters to save them from the boring Teredo worm—hence the saying "a copper-bottomed investment".

The railway came in 1869, and was the steepest unassisted railway track in the world with a gradient of 1 in 27. But it did not help the valley regain its prosperity of the late 1700's.

Greenfield also had a wire-works, a foundry, woollen-mill and copper-bolt works. The noise and the smell must have been incredible. Yet today you can drive past this once thriving industrial community without even knowing it had been there. The Greenfield Valley Heritage Park preserves what is left and runs many interesting events in the summer months.

A booklet entitled *History of the Greenfield Valley* by Dr. Ken Davies is available from the park's visitor centre. Tel (01352) 714172 **www.greenfieldvalley.com**

Appendix
Directory of Resources

All entries correct at time of going to print, but may change. While these are all tried and recommended references, the author does not necessarily agree with *all* the opinions expressed by different authors or websites listed here. Suggestions for future additions to this list are welcomed at info@northwalesbutterflies.org.uk

Books

Bob Flowerdew's Complete Book of Companion Planting.

Welsh Verse, Translations by Tony Conran, published by Seren

John Clare, Selected Poems, Everyman's Poetry ed. By R.K.R.Thornton, Orion Publishing.

Gerard Manley Hopkins: The Major Works (Oxford World's Classics) Oxford University Press

Hopkins Society, secretary; I. Jones, 41 North Drive, Rhyl LL18 4SW, tel; 01745 354 151 **www.hopkinsoc.freeserve.co.uk**

Gwen Tomos and **Rhys Lewis, minister of Bethel** by Daniel Owen

How to Make a Wildlife Garden by Chris Baines – the bible on this subject.

Chris Packham's Back Garden Nature Reserve published by the Wildlife Trusts.

Gardening for Butterflies by Jan Miller, to be published in 2006

The History of the parishes of Whiteford and Holywell by Thomas Pennant, 1796, facsimile version published 1988 by Clwyd Library service, contains a biography of Pennant by Dr. Paul Evans.

Saving Butterflies, ed Dunbar, pub. Butterfly Conservation – excellent
advice on managing and enhancing different habitats

Britain's Butterflies by Still and Tomlinson, many photos from different
angles plus all their caterpillars, pupae and eggs, this and above available from
Butterfly Conservation Head Office or from
info@northwalesbutterflies.org.uk tel 01352 711198

Field Guide to the Moths of great Britain and Northern Ireland by
Paul Waring and M. Townsend, illustrated by R. Lewington. – paintings of
all the British macro moths in life position.

Colour Identification Guide to Moths of the British Isles by B.Skinner
pub. Viking– photos of all the British macro moths as pinned museum
specimens.

Wild Flowers of Britain and Ireland by Fitter and Fitter, illustrated by M.
Blamey – the standard reference to all British wildflowers with colour
paintings of each.

Field Guide to the Bumblebees of Great Britain and Ireland by M.
Edwards and M. Jenner, pub. Ocelli 2005

Complete Guide to British Insects by M. Chinery, pub. Collins – photos
of all groups of insects that the keen amateur naturalist is likely to see in the
British Isles.

Natural History Museum Guides to British Fossils – the best
comprehensive guides to all the fossils found in Britain, in three inexpensive
paperback volumes;
British Caenozoic Fossils (Tertiary and Quaternary)
British Mesozoic Fossils
British Palaeozoic Fossils
Published by Intercept Ltd. (used copies available from www. Amazon.com)

Identification charts

The Field Studies Council publishes excellent simple, laminated, colour, pocket ID charts for a lot of different kinds of wildlife; see **www.field-studies-council.org** or telephone 01743 852140. FSC publications, Preston Montfort, Shrewsbury SY4 1HW. Also contact them for booklet of courses run at centres all over the UK and abroad.

Butterflies of North Wales ID chart (pub. 2006) available from **www.northwalesbutterflies.org.uk** or tel 01352 711198. On this website you can also find a chart of common garden species to print off from the Education pages, an online ID workshop plus photos and details of all North Wales species and recording forms on this website. Butterfly and moth records needed!

British Bumblebees ID cards shown in this book (AppleMac format) from Carl Clee, Natural History Centre (Liverpool Museum)
William Brown Street
Liverpool
L3 8EN
0151 4784291
Also a more detailed set to print off from the Natural History Museum website at; **www.nhm.ac.uk**/entomology/bombus/bumblebeeid.html

Bumblebee recorders wanted by the
National Bumblebee Survey Project Officer
Buglife – tel 01733 201213 or e-mail; edie.jolley@buglife.org.uk
www.buglife.org.uk

Magazines

British Wildlife The Old Dairy, Milton on Stour, Gillingham, Dorset SP8 5PX.
Tel; 01747 835511. **www.britishwildlife.com** excellent bi-monthly, subscription magazine covering up to date reports on all aspects of British natural history and conservation.

Natur Cymru *A Review of Wildlife in Wales*
Natur Cymru
Maes y Ffynnon
Penrhosgarnedd
Bangor
Gwynedd
LL57 2DW Tel: 01248 385574
written by and for people who care about the Welsh environment. It is
available by subscription. **www.naturcymru.org.uk**

Natural World Wales (Wales Wildlife Trusts) tel 01733288119
www.wildlifetrusts.org

Biodiversity News, 1/10 Kite Zone, Temple Quay House, Bristol BS1 6EB
tel; 0117 372 6276 e-mail; biodiversitynews@defra.gsi.gov.uk – the DEFRA
newsletter for Biodiversity Action Partnerships. **www.ukbap.org.uk**

"Y Naturiaethwr" Welsh-language natural history journal,
Editor; G.Wynne, "Gwylfa", Licsm, Treffynnon, Sir Fflint CH8 8NQ
www.cymdeithasedwardllwyd.org.uk

"Out and About" –each year a programme of countryside events in
Denbighshire is available free from Loggerheads Country Park, tel 01352
810614, or see **www.denbighshire.gov.uk**

Most other County Councils also publish free newsletters and events lists.

Cambria – bi-monthly Welsh news, culture, history and lifestyle. Available
from newsagents or by subscription, **tel;**01267 290188 **fax:**01267 290188
www.cambriamagazine.com
Cambria Magazine, PO Box 22, Carmarthen SA32 7YH

Library Services

(All have lists of local societies, colleges, leaflets on local nature reserves, courses, events, etc.)
Flintshire Library Service to print new or facsimile editions; Community Librarian Mold, Library Museum and Gallery, Earl Road, Mold, 01352 754791
e-mail; Gillian_Fraser@flintshire.gov.uk

Denbighshire Library Service; tel; 01824 708200

Conwy Borough Council Library Service;
llyfr.lib.pencadlys.hq@conwy.gov.uk
Tel: (01492) 576140 Fax: (01492) 592061

Anglesey, Conwy and Gwynnedd Library Services
www.ynysmon.gov.uk/english/library/talnet.htm

County Councils

(All County Councils have Country Parks open to the public, free historical and wildlife events for children and adults, Local Biodiversity Action Plans (LBAPs) and all kinds of related information.)

Isle of Anglesey County Council, Council Offices,
Llangefni, Anglesey. LL77 7TW
01248 750057

Gwynedd Council, Council Offices, Caernarfon, Gwynedd. LL55 1SH.
Phone (01286) 672255 Fax (01286) 673993
www.gwynedd.gov.uk

Denbighshire County Council
County Hall
Wynnstay Road
Ruthin
LL15 1YN
01824 706000

Denbighshire Customer Services; 01824 706 555
www.denbighshire.gov.uk
Flintshire County Council
County Hall
Mold
Flintshire CH7 6NB
01352 752121
www.Flintshire.gov.uk

Wrexham County Borough Council
The Guildhall
Wrexham
LL11 1AY
Tel: 01978 292000
www.wrexham.gov.uk

Powys County Council,
Powys County Hall,
Llandrindod Wells,
Powys
LD1 5LG.
Tel: 01597 826000
www.powys.gov.uk

Email the Secretary of State for Wales at
wales.office@wales.gsi.gov.uk

Local Natural History Societies and Parks

Butterfly Conservation North Wales Branch;
Website; **www.northwalesbutterflies.org.uk**, e-mail;
info@northwalesbutterflies.org.uk or tel; 01352 711198
Sec; Julian Thompson, Pensychnant Conservation Centre, Sychnant Pass,
Conwy LL32 8BJ, tel 01492 592595 (Pensychnant Conservation centre also
run their own programme of events)

Butterfly Conservation Wales Office; 10 Calvert Terrace, Swansea SA1 5AR tel; 0870 7706 153 e-mail; info.bcw@btconnect.com

Butterfly Conservation Head Office; Manor Yard, East Lulworth, Wareham, Dorset BH20 5QP tel; 0870 7744309, e-mail info@butterfly-conservation.org Reg, charity no. 254937
www.butterfly-conservation.org

Cymdeithas Edward Llwyd, Cymdithas Genedlaethol Naturiaethwyr Cymru Iwan Roberts,Yr Ysgrifennydd Aelodaeth, 3 Rhes y Rheilffordd, Rhuthun,
Sir Ddinbych LL15 1BT (Welsh language natural history society)

Wales Biodiversity Partership website **www.biodiversitywales.org.uk** or in welsh is **www.biodiversitywales.org.uk/cymraeg**

Friends of Pistyll Gwyn Quarry, Sec. tel; 01824 780684, or john@shakesby1.fsnet.co.uk

North Wales Bat Group, tel; 01745 540360, e-mail; mike.castle@which.net

Clwyd Badger Group, PO Box 708, Mold Post Office, Mold, Flintshire CH7 2AA, tel; 01244 544823

North Wales Wildlife Trust; has a large number of reserves across the region, plus local events programme and newsletter.
Head Office, 376 High St., Bangor, Gwynedd LL57 1YE

Denbighshire Council Countryside Service
For "Out and About" walks and events booklet, or from Loggerheads Country Park visitor centre; tel;01352 810614
www.denbighshire.gov.uk/biodiversity for info. on wildlife in Denbighshire. If you would like to be sent these biodiversity pages as a booklet please contact Biodiversity Team, Denbighshire Countryside Service, Old Gaol, Ruthin, Denbighshire. Tel: 01824 708263 / 8234

The Friends of Greenfield Valley, Greenfield Valley Heritage Park,
Greenfield, Holywell. Flintshire. CH8 7GH
Tel: (01352) 714172
www.greenfieldvalley.com
Have a varied programme of family events including butterfly walks, bat
nights, local industrial history and a farm park.

Llanarmon yn Ial Conservation Society
T. Rigby 01824 780408

Dyserth and District Field Club
Take guided local walks every two weeks, with lectures in winter and coach
excursions in summer. Experts in all kinds of natural history and archaeology
are on hand to show members the treasures of our local countryside.
Telephone 01745 570405 for more details

**Deeside Urban Wildlife Group (Now renamed "North East Wales
Wildlife" or NEWwildlife)**
Have a volunteer membership who manage local reserves and go on guided
walks and surveys. Also paid staff who do much work with local schools and
running environmental training courses for professionals
Email; weo@duwg.org.uk Telephone; 01244 541005

The Three Rivers Project
Volunteers carry out conservation work, including building artificial otter
holts along many rivers in North-east Wales. If you would like to help
contact bettylee_uk@yahoo.com or tel; 01244 550993

Froglife
Mansion House, Halesworth, Suffolk IP19 8AY tel; 01986 873733
www.froglife.org info. on wildlife ponds, amphibians, etc.

The Friends of Anglesey Red Squirrels
Llys Goferydd, Bryn Cefni Industrial estate, Llangefni, Anglesey LL77 7XA
www.redsquirrels.info/main.html

The Friends of Treborth Botanic Garden

A monthly moth group meets at Treborth Botanical Gardens, Bangor.
as well as many local plant enthusiasts.
University of Wales, Bangor LL57 2RQ
Tel (01248 353398) **www.treborthbotanicgarden.org**

Buglife

The Invertebrate Conservation Trust
170A Park Road, Peterborough PE1 2UF. 01733 201213
www.buglife.org.uk

The National Council for the Conservation of Plants and Gardens (NCCPG)

Protects and conserves Britain's Garden Plants by organising 'National
Collections' of plants, in the care of ordinary gardens and gardeners,
throughout the country, and by propagating and distributing plants The
North Wales Group of the NCCPG meet at Bod Erw Hotel, A55 at St.
Asaph on the second Tuesday of each month.

For further information and a current programme of events, contact, either:
Chairman: David Toyne e-mail; david-toyne@beeb.net or telephone: 01978
790576 or: Secretary: Terry Scheers Telephone: 01492 531036

NCCPG National Office

The Stable Courtyard, Wisley Garden, Woking, Surrey GU23 6QP Tel:
01483 211465 Fax: 01483 212404

Country Parks

Alyn Water Country Park, Wrexham Tel: 01978 762122

Mold Road, Gwersyllt, Wrexham LL11 4AG
Email: countryparks@wrexham.gov.uk
The largest Country Park in the Wrexham area, Alyn Waters is situated in
the beautiful Alyn Valley. Woodland, grassland and riverside walksThere is a
Visitor Centre with exhibitions on the history and wildlife of the area.
Throughout the year the Countryside Service runs an exciting programme
of events and activities, for children and adults.

Nant Mill Visitor Centre
Rhosberse Road, Coedpoeth, Wrexham LL11 3BT. Tel: 01978 752772
Email: countryparks@wrexham.gov.uk

Loggerheads Country Park, Mold
On the A494 Mold – Ruthin road
Website being redeveloped at time of going to print, but get web info via
www.denbighshire.gov.uk.
Denbighshire Countryside Service, Tel: 01352 810614
Loggerheads Country Park, Nr. Mold, Denbighshire CH7 5LH

www.clwydianrangeaonb.org.uk lots of information about places to go
and organised events in the Clwydian Hill Range, Area of Outstanding
Natural Beauty.
www.deevalleywalks.com gives detailed info. on walks between Corwen
and Llangollen.
Leaflet also available from Tourist offices.
www.walesontheweb.org has lists of all local societies and natural history
organisations.
www.bbc.co.uk/nature/animals/wildbritain
great BBC website with all kinds of wildlife information.

Local History Societies and resources

Gwrych Castle Preservation Trust
Tel; 01745 857139 (leave message)
7Clive Avenue, Prestatyn LL19 7BL, Denbighshire.
www.gwrychtrust.co.uk

Flintshire Historical Society
Secretary, 69 Pen-y-Maes Avenue, Rhyl, Denbighshire LL18 4ED
Tel: 01745 332220

St. Asaph Archaeology Society
Secretary,67 Ashley Court, St Asaph LL17 0PL

Greenfield Valley Heritage Park
Greenfield, Holywell. Flintshire. CH8 7GH Telephone: (01352) 714172
www.greenfieldvalley.com
The valley is now both an industrial archaeology and a wildlife park. They run a varied programme of family events including historical walks and lectures, butterfly walks, bat nights and a farm park.

Parys Mountain Copper Mines, Anglesey
In the 18th century the largest copper mine in the world, with great importance to British economy and the slave trade. Unfortunately, there is currently no public access into mines, but there is a footpath around the top of Parys Mountain, details of which are provided on a leaflet, which is available at the public car park on the mountain. There is an exhibition of artefacts recovered from the mine at The Sail Loft in Amlwch port.
Grid Reference: SH439905
Contact details: Anglesey Mining plc, Parys Mountain, Amlwch, Anglesey, LL68 9RE, UK. Excellent website with lots of info:
www.parysmountain.co.uk

Cambrian Archaeological Association
Membership Sec; Frances Lynch Llewellyn, Halfway House, Pont y Pandy, Halfway Bridge, Bangor LL57 3DG
Email: f.m.lynch@btopenworld.com, Tel: 01248 364 865
The national archaeological society of Wales. Organises field meetings. Publishes the journal 'Archaeologia Cambrensis'. Provides some funding for research. For Grant applications contact the General Secretary, 28 Gipsy Lane, Exmouth, EX8 3HN

Young Archaeologists Club and Clwydian Range project
Tel Fiona Gale 01824 708262 or e-mail fiona.gale@denbighshire.gov.uk

Welsh Historic Gardens Trust
Secretary, Ty Len, Talybont, Ceredigion, SY24 5ER
(has a North Wales Branch)

The Welsh Language Initiative
Terrig House, Chester Street, Mold. tel; 01352 755614 or see;
www.welshfolkdance.org.uk

National Trust Office for Wales
Trinity Square, Llandudno LL30 2DE **www.nationaltrust.org.uk**
or tel. 01492 860123

Thomas Pennant Group
A pack of guide leaflets of "Pennant Walks"and information about
The Pennant Group is available from; N. Closs-Parry, Bryn Ceris, Carmel,
Holywell CH8 7DD. Tel; 01352 711036 or Paul Brighton; 01352 712588

www.britannia.com/wales lots of info. incl Welsh history, literature, places
to visit and all things cultural
www.cpat.org.uk Clwyd/Powys archaeological Trust
www.wrexham.gov.uk/english/heritage/holt_castle.htm
information about Holt Castle.

Gathering the Jewels website www.gtj.org.uk
A wonderful resource of Welsh culture and history; over 20,000 images of
objects, books, letters, aerial photographs and other items from museums,
libraries and record offices in Wales.

www.archaeology.co.uk has a directory of all local archaeological
societies in the UK and how to go on a dig in archaeology. Or write
to;Current Archaeology, 9 Nassington Road, London, NW3 2TX tel; 08456
44 77 07
www.naturedetectives.org.uk excellent resources for children and schools
www.megalithic.co.uk maps of all megalithic sites with information.
www.historicchurches.org.uk – lots of info about fascinating historic
church buildings all over the UK.

Geology

RIGS (Regionally Important Geological Sites) publish geological guides to a number of local towns; contact the Geodiversity Officer, c/o Millennium Ecocentre, Borras Airfield, Tarmac, Holt Road, Wrexham LL13 9SE. tel; 01978 361543

Or e-mail j.malpas@chester.ac.uk Website; **www.ukrigs.org**
www.bgs.ac.uk website of the British Geological Survey has all kinds of general interest information about rocks.

Botany

Botanical Society of the British Isles

For information about our wild flowers, field trips, courses, an online identification key and lots more see **www.bsbi.org.uk** or write to Mr R. Gwynn Ellis, 41 Marlborough Road, Roath, Cardiff, CF23 5BU. From whom the contact details for the local botanical Recorders are available. The BSBI Botanical Recorder for Denbighshire is Dr. Jean Green, tel;01745 730254 or e-mail; jean@coedduon.fsworld.co.uk

Record your elm data

The information gathered from the Elm Map project and walks will be stored on The Ancient Tree Hunt website. Join an Elm Map walk or enter your elm discoveries online at **www.ancient-tree-hunt.org.uk**. A full list of Elm Map walks is available from the Ramblers' Association at
www.ramblers.org.uk.
Ancient Tree Hunt
c/o The Woodland Trust
Autumn Park, Dysart Road
Grantham, Lincolnshire NG11 6LL. Tel: 01476 581111

Information on Ragwort; www.butterfly-conservation.org/ne/news/ragwort/index.html
English Nature Information note; Common ragwort *Senecio jacobea*
Towards a ragwort management strategy by John Bacon Senior Land Manager, Dr Richard Jefferson. Grassland Ecologist, Dr David Sheppard, Invertebrate Ecologist

Terrestrial Wildlife Team, English Nature, 11 June 2003
Tel: 01733 455243
English Nature, Northminster House, Peterborough PE1 1UA

Fungi
British Mycological Society

Joseph Banks Building, Royal Botanic Gardens, Kew, Richmond, Surrey
TW9 3AB e-mail members@britmycolsoc.org.uk. Organises an annual
programme of scientific meetings, workshops and forays all over the country.
www.fungus.org.uk and go to North West Fungus group—lots of pictures
and ID help.

Products
Agralan Ltd

Many products for the organic and wildlife gardener, including wooden
Bumblebee nestboxes; The Old Brickyard, Ashton Keynes, Swindon,
Wiltshire SN6 6QRTel: (01285) 860015 Fax: (01285) 860056
www.agralan.co.uk

Wiggly Wigglers

Sell wormeries, bird food and insect nest boxes, wild plants, books on
wildlife gardening tel;01981 500391 Fax 01981 500108
www.wigglywigglers.co.uk
Lower Blakemere Farm, Blakemere, Herefordshire HR2 9PX

Alana Ecology

Sell every kind of supply for the naturalist and wildlife enthusiast, from GPS
to moth traps. Tel: 01588 630173 or **www.alanaecology.com**

Miller-Klein Associates, sustainability consultancy
www.miller-klein.com

Wildlife Garden Plants and seeds

www.northwalesbutterflies.org.uk

Sells all the British species of butterfly and moth larval foodplants as well as many unusual garden plants to attract butterflies to your garden. (seeds also available) Or tel 01352 711198 for a catalogue. Also attracting many other insects like Bumblebees for pollination of fruit crops and predators of pests. A garden design service is available for a butterfly and other wildlife-friendly gardens. Part of the profits go to the North Wales Branch of Butterfly Conservation.

Government Agencies

Countryside Council for Wales /Cyngor Cefn Gwald (CCW)

Tel;01352 706600 and Swyddog Cadwraeth - Tir Gofal scheme (countryside stewardship for farmers)

Glan y Nant, Unit 19, Mold Business Park, Wrexham Road, Mold, Flintshire CH7 1XP Glan y Nant, Uned 19, Parc Busnes, Ffordd Wrecsam,Yr Wyddgrug, Sir Fflint, CH7 1XP Ffon/Tel: 01352 706600 Ffacs/Fax: 01352 752346

Secretary of State for Wales

wales.office@wales.gsi.gov.uk or write to; The Chief Executive, Bodlondeb, Conwy.

DEFRA (used to be Ministry of Agriculture Fisheries and Food) website; **www.defra.gov.uk**

Environment Agency Wales

Tel; 08459 333111 or email; enquiries@environment-agency.gov.uk

Coed Cymru tel; 01824 708265 or 01352 703261

Planning Dept., Trem Clwyd, Canol y Dre, Ruthin LL15 1QA

Annual Local Country Festivals

North Wales Garden Festival

On the Sunday and Monday of May and August Bank holidays at Bodelwyddan Castle, on the A55 near Abergele.

WoodFest

Woodcraft to buy as well as advice on using your own woodland; every June at St. Asaph; see **www.woodfest.co.uk** or Telephone: 01745 585929

Cadi Ha

Celebrations take place on the first Saturday in May in Holywell, Bagillt, Flint and Caerwys. More information from; The Welsh Language Initiative, Terrig House, Chester Street, Mold. tel; 01352 755614 or see **www.welshfolkdance.org.uk**

Agricultural shows

Held in many towns, including

The Denbigh Show, The Ruthin Show and the Anglesey Show all in August

The Llandegla Festival, usually early September.

The Denbighshire Walking Festival usually mid-September

Find out more from local County Councils websites or enquiry tel. nos.

Wales Wildlife Week

Usually 2nd or 3rd week of June; events for children and adults at many places across north Wales. For info see **www.biodiversitywales.org.uk** or in welsh is **www.biodiversitywales.org.uk/cymraeg**. or telephone 01352 810614

Farmers Markets

Northop near Mold

Every third Sunday of the month at the North Wales Horticultural College

Colwyn Bay

Weekly event every Thursday between June and December. Held at Bay

View Shopping Centre Car Park. A wide range of fresh local produce on offer 9am-2pm weather permitting, contact 01492 531764

For other Farmers Markets, and other festivals see **www.north-wales-events.co.uk**

Crafts

Basket-making Courses

All materials provided for beginners; tel; Mandy Coates 01745 833742

Woodcraft courses

Peter Boyd, wood carving courses and commissions; tel; 01248 602102, Hendre Hall, Tal y Bont, Bangor LL57 3YP, jctn 12 off A55.

Various courses including coracle making, coppicing techniques, etc. are occasionally run at The Warren, Bodfari; tel; 01745 710626

Philip Snow BA

Wildlife Art & Illustration. 2 Beach Cottages   Malltraeth   Anglesey LL62 5AT Tel: 01407 840512.

Elizabeth Gleave

Designer of guide leaflets and interpretation panels
eagleave@boltblue.com

www.craft-show.co.uk list craft shows all over the UK plus the craftspeople who are attending.

Local Colleges

Teaching short courses in natural history and country craft with no previous qualifications or knowledge required, as well as professional training courses;

Plas Tan y Bwlch

Maentwrog, Blaenau Ffestiniog, Gwynedd LL41 3YU Tel; 0871 8714004 0
Tel: 0871 8714004 14004 **www.plastanybwlch.com**

Rhyd-y-creuau Field Studies Centre
The Drapers' Field Centre, Betws-y-coed, Conwy LL24 0HB
Tel: 01690 710494   Fax: 01690 710458
Email: enquiries.rc@field-studies-council.org

Llysfasi Agricultural College
Ruthin, Denbighshire LL15 2LB
Tl; 01978 790263 Fax: 01978 790 468 Email: admin@llysfasi.ac.uk

Wrexham Training
(Part of Coleg Llysfasi), Felin Puleston, Ruabon Road, Wrexham LL13 7RF
Phone: 01978 363 033 Fax: 01978 362959 Email: wtadmin@llysfasi.ac.uk